The Seven Practices of Mentally Superior Athletes

Once athletes reach the highest levels of competition in college and professional sports, the mental aspect of the game becomes increasingly vital to performance. *The Seven Practices of Mentally Superior Athletes* is a short and snappy reference text intended for repeated use that explains the importance of the mental side of the game and offers concise advice for improvement. Wald outlines the most important sport psychology skills in a way that can be easily understood and applied to athletes regardless of what sport they play. It also features illustrative stories that demonstrate exactly how these skills can be applied on the field, court, course, or arena.

This book is particularly helpful to busy athletes with demanding lifestyles. It will also be useful for coaches who want to continue their education and learn more about sport psychology and how to implement these mental training habits with their athletes.

Dr. Raphi Wald, PsyD, ABN, CMPC, is a Florida licensed psychologist. He is a certified mental performance consultant and board-certified neuropsychologist. He serves as the Team Psychologist for Florida Atlantic University and Lynn University.

The Seven Practices of Mentally Superior Athletes

A Brief Guide to Harnessing Skills from Sport Psychology

Raphi Wald

Routledge
Taylor & Francis Group

NEW YORK AND LONDON

First published 2019
by Routledge
605 Third Avenue, New York, NY 10017

and by Routledge
4 Park Square, Milton Park, Abingdon, Oxon OX14 4RN

First issued in paperback 2022

Routledge is an imprint of the Taylor & Francis Group, an informa business

© 2019 Taylor & Francis

Library of Congress Cataloging-in-Publication Data
Names: Wald, Raphi, author.
Title: The seven habits of mentally effective athletes : a brief guide to
   harnessing skills from sport psychology / Dr. Raphi Wald.
Description: New York, NY : Routledge, 2019.
Identifiers: LCCN 2018042734 (print) | LCCN 2018047072 (ebook) |
   ISBN 9780429024542 (Ebook) | ISBN 9780367110598 (hardback)
Subjects: LCSH: Athletes—Psychology—Handbooks, manuals, etc. |
   Sports—Psychological aspects—Handbooks, manuals, etc. |
   Mental health—Handbooks, manuals, etc.
Classification: LCC GV706.4 (ebook) | LCC GV706.4 .W34 2019
   (print) | DDC 796.01—dc23
LC record available at https://lccn.loc.gov/2018042734

ISBN 13: 978-1-03-247583-7 (pbk)
ISBN 13: 978-0-367-11059-8 (hbk)
ISBN 13: 978-0-429-02454-2 (ebk)

DOI: 10.4324/9780429024542

Typeset in Times New Roman
by Apex CoVantage, LLC

Contents

Acknowledgments

My most important acknowledgment is without a doubt for the unending love and support provided to me by my wife Dayna. There is no way I would be where I am without you. My beautiful children Layla, Joey, and Evan are also an unending source of inspiration.

Looking back on my career to this point I have had the benefit of having tremendous mentors along the way. Had any one of them not been in place I am sure that I would not have the knowledge base to write this book. This includes Dr. Louis Shuster at Tufts University, Robert Nelson at UMass Boston, Dr. Wallace Deckel at University of Connecticut Health Center, and Dr. Mark Todd at the Neurological Institute at North Broward Medical Center.

I would also like to thank all of the athletic trainers, coaches, administrative staff, strength coaches, and equipment staff at both Lynn University and Florida Atlantic University. There are way too many of you to identify by name, but you make my job easy with the support you provide. I would not trade my experiences at these universities for any others.

Introduction

It's okay to say it . . . sports do matter. Sure, athletes aren't curing cancer or bringing about world peace, but they are nonetheless important. Anyone who says that sports don't matter just don't get it.

First, there are numerous benefits to sports. Athletics help people stay in shape (crucial in this age of childhood obesity), improve the ability to work with a team, improve self-esteem, lower the risk of substance use, and lower the risk of depression. That should be enough to convince anyone, but if it isn't, consider the escape that sports provide for millions of people worldwide. Watching and participating in sports provide a healthy break from the many stresses of life. If sports didn't matter, would tens of thousands of people spend their hard-earned money to see them in person every day? Would older men and women, the weekend warriors, continue to compete in leagues despite increased risk of injury as we age?

Many people also devote their lives to sports. This includes athletes, coaches, athletic trainers, athletic directors, and countless other administrators who make the game on the field or the court possible. For many of these people, their livelihoods depend on winning and losing. You'd better believe that sports matter for them.

Professional sports also give people a sense of local and national pride. Consider the Boston Marathon bombing in 2013. On that date, terrorists left bombs near the finish line of the marathon that killed three people and injured many others. However, it brought the city of Boston together in an incredible way. Bostonians adopted the slogan "Boston Strong." That season, the Boston Red Sox hung a jersey in their dugout with the number 617 (the Boston area code) on the back. The team won the World Series that year and helped the city heal as much as any sports team could. The Red Sox provided a level of escape and happiness to the area that was invaluable.

Similarly, following the September 11th attacks in 2001, the New York Yankees and New York Mets provided a much-needed distraction for the residents of New York when play resumed approximately a week later. Later that season, the president of the United States threw out the first pitch at a Yankees game, which underscored the importance of unity in our country.

Having established the importance of athletics, what do we now do with that information? Within sports, as in many other areas of life, we are constantly striving to be better. The golfer who shoots 75 wants to shoot par. The scratch golfer wants to shoot in the 60s. The 75-year-old golfer wants to shoot his age.

The area of sport psychology is relatively new. There is also no one correct definition of what a mental skills coach or sport psychologist is. Some of these professionals have a background in kinesiology and bring a strong understanding of human movement and exercise to the field. Others are former athletes who use their experiences from participating in sport. Still others such as myself come from the field of psychology. Originally, as a licensed psychologist, I specialized in the diagnosis and treatment of psychiatric illnesses such as depression and anxiety. I further specialized in the field of neuropsychology, the field that studies the connection between brain function, behavior, and cognition (thinking skills such as focus and memory), gaining my board certification in this area.

Over time in practice, I grew more interested in sport psychology as I treated more and more athletes with psychological, cognitive, and performance problems. Despite already being a practicing psychologist and neuropsychologist, I wanted to learn as much as possible about the field so as to provide the best possible help for my clients. This led me to complete a course of study that culminated in my certification as a CMPC (certified mental performance consultant).

My background as a psychologist and neuropsychologist has been an immense help to me in improving myself as a sport psychologist. Sport performance issues present in a number of different ways. On occasion, some athletes are functioning well emotionally with no underlying psychological issues but find themselves performing significantly below expectation. For this type of individual, perhaps using purely performance-based approaches would be most helpful to get them functioning at their best. Still other competitors scuffle on the field or court as a result of a psychological problem such as depression, anxiety, or a relationship issue. For these individuals, addressing the underlying issues appropriately based on best practices and research may best resolve their problems. Finally, some athletes have difficulty as a result of both psychological and performance-based problems. This may require some combination of different approaches to resolve fully.

The bottom line here is that everyone needs something different. I have been fortunate enough to have a background that allows me to cover the full spectrum of psychological, cognitive, and performance-based issues. I also feel very fortunate to work as the Team Psychologist for Florida Atlantic University in Boca Raton and Lynn University in Boca Raton. Their athletic departments have been wonderful places to work. They have always done everything in their power to provide support to me in any way necessary for the sake of their student athletes. I have been fortunate enough to work in all sports at both of these schools including soccer, basketball, track and field, cross country, swimming, diving, volleyball, sand volleyball, baseball, softball, football, lacrosse, tennis, and golf. I have also had the good fortune to work within the world of professional sports, most extensively professional baseball.

The seven practices of mentally superior athletes is based on my experiences working as a sport psychologist in various capacities in NCAA Division 1, NCAA Division II, and professional sports. While stories provided in this book may be in one sport, the concepts are applicable in any athletic area. Further, while the book focuses on sports, the concepts presented can be applied almost anywhere, including in business and in the performing arts. The illustrative stories are all based on real experiences, but significant details have been changed so as to protect the identity of clients.

This book is fairly short and meant to be easily digestible and accessible for coaches and athletes who need help on the fly. It is meant to be read multiple times as a sport performance bible of sorts. While it is impossible to be perfectly mentally superior, this book should put you in the best possible position to gain a crucial edge in the ferociously competitive world of sports.

1 Deal with Underlying Psychological Problems (Mental Health)

Depression and anxiety are performance killers. When understanding emotional distress, it is important to bear in mind both the biological and learned components. Depression and anxiety are among the most common psychological or medical problems globally. Why? Part of the answer is because almost everyone has the potential to become anxious and depressed. This potential lays dormant in us, and if a stress emerges in our lives, it can kick this dormant potential into an active state. For some people, this potential is minimal, and only a major stress such as a major traumatic accident or the death of a loved one can activate it. For others, this potential is more easily activated. For these individuals, a fight with a coach can be sufficient. Once such negative emotional problems are kicked into action, the original cause may not matter anymore. In other words, even if the original problem is resolved, the feelings of sadness and worry are already off and running and continue despite this resolution. Unfortunately, what most people who have never experienced true severe depression or anxiety cannot fully understand is that you cannot always "just suck it up" or "just get over it." Would you ask a person with epilepsy or diabetes to "just suck it up"? Depression and anxiety can be every bit as debilitating as physical illnesses. In fact, if you ask a person with true severe depression if they would be willing to trade the depression for diabetes or epilepsy, you might be surprised to find that quite often, the answer is yes.

Many people struggling with emotional distress are not surprised to hear of the clear biological components involved in sadness and worry. They realize that their mother, father, aunt, uncle, or cousin has had depression or "is a worrier." Nowhere is the connection between emotion and biology more apparent than in the physical complaints that come along with psychological difficulties. Gastroesophageal reflux disease, migraine headaches, stress headaches, joint pain, back pain, and susceptibility to infection are among the numerous physical problems that can accompany emotional problems. Pain that is associated with psychological distress is one of many ways that performance can be inhibited by problems with mood or excessive worry. There is a part of your brain that, when you are distressed, communicates with the rest of your body in order to release a hormone that is damaging to your body and immune system.

Further, it is also important to note that very rarely does a person experience true depression in the absence of any anxiety, or true anxiety in the absence of any depression. The two are most often inseparable to some degree. If you are constantly worrying, you probably will be feeling somewhat depressed about how worried you are. On the flip side, if you are extremely depressed, you are likely to be somewhat worried about the implications of that sadness.

What is depression technically? It is the presence of a group of five or more symptoms. Most often, when a patient comes into my office and is depressed, they already know without requiring a professional to tell them. Many of my patients have described it as "everything being dark," "everything is hard to do, it's hard just to stand up," or "every second is miserable." As with most things in the field of psychology, it operates along a range of severity from extremely mild to severe. While one person might feel "unfocused or unmotivated" at one end of the spectrum, another might be having active thoughts of hurting themselves in order to end their pain or punish themselves. With the stresses that professional and collegiate athletes face, it is not surprising that they often have these sorts of problems.

What, then, is anxiety? Anxiety, simply defined, is excess worry. It occurs when a person worries more than is appropriate given a certain circumstance. This worry can come in numerous forms that express themselves based on a person's biology, life experiences, and personality. Among the most common expressions of anxiety that are diagnosed by mental health professionals are generalized anxiety, panic attacks, and obsessive-compulsive disorder (although OCD is now technically viewed as a separate issue).

Generalized anxiety is what most people probably think of when they think of anxiety. You worry. If you consider yourself a "worrier," then you may lie somewhere along this spectrum of excessive worry, even if your struggles are not severe enough to warrant a clinical diagnosis. These worries often occupy your mind much of the day and drain your psychological energy more than they should, leaving nothing for the field or court.

Meanwhile, panic attacks are a different and very distressing expression of excessive worry. Despite what many people think, they are quite common. They involve a group of both mental and physical symptoms, including feeling like you are dying, feeling like you are losing control, increased heart rate, excessive sweating, shortness of breath, feeling like you are choking, and dizziness, among several others. Feelings of panic are common in athletes. Many times, they come in response to something stressful, such as an extended hitting slump, and many times they come about for no reason at all. In other instances, they appear because you are worried about the potential for having one. Why do they happen? Panic attacks are simply a misinterpretation by your body. The symptoms of panic are quite similar to those that you would experience if you were in a life-threatening situation, like being trapped in a cage with a tiger. Your heart rate would increase, your body would pay less attention to processes that occur during relaxation such as digesting food, and blood would rush to your muscles in order to help you take action. However, during panic attacks, your life is not in danger. During a panic attack your mind and body act as though they are in danger, even though they are not.

The third of these anxiety-related disorders consists of obsessions and compulsions and is called obsessive-compulsive disorder. Obsessions are a disproportionate preoccupation with an object or idea; compulsions are repetitive acts that are aimed at relieving those obsessions. The acts are often not linked to the obsessions in a realistic way. For example, an obsession might be a person spending most of their day worrying that their house will be broken into. The compulsion might be tapping on the doorpost a hundred times before leaving the house in order to stop that from happening. It is important to differentiate rituals and superstitions that many athletes have from true compulsions.

Often, a person must decide themselves if their feelings of worry or sadness are severe enough to warrant considerable attention or treatment. This is the way that many psychological disorders work. Both the mental health professional and the individual must decide if there is "clinically significant distress." In other words, are these problems interfering with your life in an appreciable way?

When this chapter speaks of psychological turmoil, it is important to keep in mind what is intended by the words "psychological problems." This book has limitations. In other words, there are psychological difficulties that go beyond the scope of this book and its contents. People who suffer from mental illnesses such as schizophrenia and bipolar disorder—difficulties that are severe and often lifelong in nature—must partner with both a psychiatrist for medical management of their illness and with a psychologist for ongoing talk therapy. While this chapter is not meant to deal specifically with the severe symptoms associated with these problems, it is my hope that it will prove helpful in coping with the feelings of distress, worry, and sadness that often have nothing to do with on-the-field issues.

More specifically, this chapter's title refers to those issues that are most often associated with anxiety disorders and depression. Whether one is actually suffering from diagnosable anxiety or depression, or less severe problems, there are techniques and habits that are helpful as evidenced by research and my own clinical experience to be effective in managing these difficulties. All of these psychological disorders are defined by a list of associated symptoms. For example, if an individual has five out of nine symptoms associated with depression (insomnia, poor appetite, feelings of guilt, etc.), then they can be clinically diagnosed with depression. However, as good psychologists and psychiatrists know, even one or two of these symptoms can be distressing. This in turn destroys performance.

While problems with depression and anxiety are the most common problems faced by athletes, they are by no means the only ones. Substance use is a very common problem as well. Many athletes think that marijuana in particular is not addictive. This could not be further from the truth! Countless promising careers have been negatively affected or completely destroyed by marijuana. Anything that feels good can be addictive.

In order to illustrate the addictive potential of marijuana, consider Jimmy, an athlete I saw in my practice. Jimmy smoked four times a day, and even woke up in the middle of the night to smoke and go back to bed. When driving long distances, he had to pack edibles so that he would not become ill from withdrawal. On one occasion, he went on a two-day cruise without first thinking about the issue of withdrawal. After a few hours on the boat, Jimmy became ill and began vomiting uncontrollably. He spent the duration of the cruise under the care of the medical staff, unable to enjoy any of the cruise activities.

If you ever find yourself making the statement "I can quit anytime I want," then it's time to take a long look in the mirror. I have had many athletes who went for substance use treatment but nonetheless failed three drug tests for marijuana, resulting in expulsion from the team and effectively ending their athletic careers. As the cliché goes, the first step is admitting you have a problem. Many people argue that pot cannot be that bad for athletes because it is legal in many places. Even still, the negative effects from pot will take their toll on a person athletically. Pot has a tendency to decrease a person's ambition, something that is crucial for those seeking to participate in Olympic or professional competition.

Drinking is a problem I find myself addressing frequently with athletes. It seems that unfortunately it has become a part of the culture of sports. If you win a big game, go on a bender. Athletes often have high tolerance for alcohol because of their physical conditioning, age, and frequency of drinking. However, if you go out drinking heavily in season, you are not only costing yourself a peak performance, but also your team. If you need treatment, please seek help from a licensed mental health professional. If you are drinking in excess in season, you're making a selfish decision that puts your team behind the eight ball.

What should an athlete do if pressures have pushed them to the point of depression, anxiety, or substance use? Be honest with yourself. There are many problems that are too big for us to handle alone. Sadness is not depression. Worry is not anxiety. Once a problem has reached a point where you and your mentors can no longer handle it alone, it is time to obtain help from a mental health professional. Mental health problems most often do not get better overnight. Find a psychologist you trust, preferably one with experience with athletes, so they can better understand your struggles. You will almost certainly find that as your mood improves, so does your game.

How do we cope with negative emotions on the field? What should we focus on when we are trying to regain composure while feeling nervous, sad, frustrated, or some other negative emotion? It can really be anything as long as it does not induce stress. For a person just beginning to hone this skill, it is typically best to use something with a great deal of depth. This may mean focusing on a great football season from high school or even a beach that you love going to in the summer. The key, however, is the depth of thought and detail involved. If the beach is your thought of choice, it will be necessary to think about all of the minor features of that beach. Where do you usually park? Is there usually already sand on the ground near the parking space? How does it feel to walk onto the sand for the first time? Is it sunny? Is it humid? Are there palm trees? What does it smell like?

In order to demonstrate how this ability looks when it is successfully utilized, I can provide an example of a 12-year-old boy I once treated who had uncontrollable obsessions relating to death. This may seem upsetting to think about. Unfortunately, obsessions are fairly common not only in adults but also children. This boy, Jimmy, thinks about death in many different ways. He worries that he will die, he worries that his parents will die, and at times he even worries that he will kill someone else, although when he is thinking clearly he knows this is something he would never do.

Jimmy desperately wishes to stop thinking in this way, although he feels that he cannot control his thoughts. These seemingly inescapable obsessions consume him so much so that he cannot go even 5 minutes without thoughts of death taking over his mind. These difficulties have interfered with his academic performance, his friendships, and his passion for baseball. He repeats to himself "don't think about death, don't think about death" but with no success. He has also begun to tap objects around him seven times in an effort to relieve these obsessive thoughts. He tells himself: "if I tap one more thing in my room seven times, then I won't die."

At a loss for answers, his parents brought him to me for help. After taking the time to understand Jimmy and his problems, I diagnosed him as having obsessive-compulsive disorder. OCD, as psychiatric illnesses go, is fairly common. The proper way to treat obsessive-compulsive disorder is by exposing the person to what they fear most while preventing them from responding with compulsions. When the problems become severe, medication can help as well.

However, as an adjunct to this treatment, I felt that it was important to help Jimmy learn to take control of his thoughts once again. Jimmy had talked to me about his love for baseball and the Florida (now Miami) Marlins. He told me that he had recordings of all of the Marlins' World Series games from their championship in 2003. The combination of the facts that Jimmy had an excellent memory and had an intense love for baseball made the Marlins the perfect tool to help him in his recovery. After learning about his passion, I asked him to tell me about the 2003 World Series. Jimmy, of course, remembered every detail. He started by telling me how every out happened in the first inning of the first game. Then he talked about how each of the runs was scored in that game. He continued in great detail all the way through the Game 6 victory for the Marlins.

Finally, at the end of his recounting of the Marlins' championship run, I asked Jimmy "how many times did you think about death during the 25 minutes you just spoke to me about the Marlins?" To this he responded "none." I also asked him "when was the last time you went 25 minutes without thinking about death?" His response was "I can't even remember."

Therein was one of the greatest keys to Jimmy's recovery. While other techniques were also important in his overcoming obsessive-compulsive disorder, the point at which he learned how to take back control of his thoughts was vital. Any time that Jimmy felt the obsessions about death coming back into his mind, he was able to "hypnotize" himself in a sense through an extreme focus on baseball and the Marlins.

However, there are many people with similar problems who cannot use this tool as effectively as Jimmy. Caryn, a mother who came to my office, was taken over by irrational worries about her two adolescent children. As they continued to grow and become more independent, she became frantically nervous that they would be kidnapped or become injured in a terrible car accident. While almost all parents worry, there reaches a point at which the worry can consume you. Caryn had reached this point and suffered from nausea in response to her seemingly uncontrollable worry. Caryn had tried shifting her focus as Jimmy had, with minimal success. Caryn found that reading, and only reading, could effectively take her mind off her excessive worries.

Of course, there were many other strategies used in psychotherapy that helped Caryn ultimately overcome her anxiety. However, when people need to find a way to "get out of their own heads," reading is typically one of the most effective ways to do so. Television is generally less effective. One can be sitting in a room with a television on and not be focused on what is happening in front of them. They may be completely consumed by their thoughts. However, reading is an active process. While reading a book and following a story line, it is much easier to force away negative thoughts. This is the reason that many people find a good book so relaxing. It is the ultimate escape from reality.

Zack Greinke

The mental health community owes a tremendous debt to Zack Greinke. Zack struggled significantly with anxiety and depression earlier in his career. Often

these two problems go hand in hand as previously discussed. When a person is extremely depressed they tend to worry in excess about a range of issues, such as when they will get better or what other people see when they interact with them. Zack struggled early on in his career because of these problems, which led to him taking a leave of absence from the game.

Think about that! He left millions of dollars on the table to try to get himself well. This move certainly paid off, because when he returned he won the Cy Young award and signed a huge contract. Some people benefit from medication, some benefit from therapy, and some need a combination of the two. Your healthcare providers can help you determine your exact treatment needs. Zack has been open about the fact that he takes an antidepressant in order to help him with his mental health. However, for the rest of the mental health community, the most important part of this episode is that he was willing to talk about it with others. His willingness to speak about his experiences has likely helped countless individuals struggling with mental illness to have hope and get treatment. Greinke's ordeal is a great example of how athletes can overcome mental illness and thrive.

2 A Penny Saved (Maintain Mental Energy)

The college track and field and cross country teams were very troubled. Often, athletes tend to date other athletes, but these track and field teams tended to stick to only other Olympic sport athletes for dating purposes. This group of 40 men and women spent a great deal of time together, as their coaches practiced them hard. Every morning they were on the track by 6 a.m., followed by lifting. They then went on their way to classes and were fortunate to ever find time to do schoolwork in the evening. This is to say nothing of how things went when they were on the road. When they traveled for meets, they had even less time to keep up with school.

Given the rigors of their schedule, these student athletes felt that they had earned the right to let loose in any way they saw fit. This typically involved binge drinking on a weekly basis and promiscuity within the group. While there were some couples among the group, they considered their relationships to be open to a large extent.

Within this context, numerous problems arose. Luke and Lindsay had been a couple for almost a year by the time their junior year rolled around. They first met early in their sophomore year when Luke transferred in. They clicked immediately, as both considered the 400-meter hurdles to be their best event. They were exclusive to each other at first, but this fell apart in time as the issue of promiscuity became more and more common among teammates. It did not take long before Luke and Lindsay found out about each other's cheating, as the group was highly prone to gossip. Secrets did not stay quiet for long.

Initially, after both were extremely hurt, they agreed that having an open relationship was the way to go. After a short time, this created a great deal of tension between Lindsay and one of her other teammates who had slept with Luke. This teammate was also now interested in Luke for the purposes of a serious, long-term relationship. Further, this issue caused a huge amount of tension between not only the two athletes but also many of the other track athletes. Gossip raged through the locker rooms and it seemed that everyone took sides. On one hand, there were those who felt Lindsay's teammate was within her right to see Luke because he and Lindsay were not exclusive. Others felt that Lindsay's teammate should have known better than to get involved with Luke.

Team trips became unbearable. Coaches always randomly placed roommates together on these trips. When teammates who were on opposite ends of this conflict stayed together, physical fights broke out at times. Distrust and anger were prevalent and performance suffered. While some team members performed well, the team as a whole began falling behind quickly.

There are clearly numerous problems with this situation. At this point in the story it is important for me to ask a question to the readers of this book: how badly do you want to excel in your sport? Is it more important than sleeping with a teammate? Is it more important than being able to binge drink? Is it more important than having an open relationship? If you answered "no" to any of these questions, you more likely have the attitude of a casual athlete— a weekend warrior.

Several aspects of this situation took away from team success. Distrust among teammates was a significant contributor. Additionally, when teammates do not like each other, they do not feel motivated to work hard for each other. This is true even in individual sports like track. If you don't like the people around you, why would you go all out for them? Alcohol is also a major problem here. You simply will not perform as well the next day if you get drunk the night before. David Wells of the New York Yankees claims he pitched a perfect game while drunk. Other baseball players have also allegedly played under the influence of drugs or alcohol. However, I would argue strongly that these are outliers. If you drink the night before a game, you are making a bad decision not only for yourself but for your entire team.

Another significant contributor to the downfall of this team is the drain that the drama caused both mentally and physically. For our purposes, think of yourself as having a specific amount of energy that you can either make a withdrawal from or deposit into, like a bank. As an athlete, you know that you will be expending a great deal of this energy on playing your sport. Soccer players will run many miles over the course of a game. Football players' bodies take a physical pounding that greatly depletes this "bank account," as the body will need time to heal and make deposits back into the account. Golfers walk a few miles during play as well. This is in addition to the mental drain that comes along with knowing that even the slightest kink in your swing could send your shot 50 yards out of bounds. Some people are energized by doing more work, however. This is where it is important to know yourself and how your body responds in different situations. Does hitting extra shots from the driving range help or hinder your performance? By the same token, some pitchers do better with an extended bullpen session prior to games, while others find it leads to poorer outcomes as it fatigues their arm. Keep a journal of your pregame routines and figure out how to maximize your mental and physical energy. Pregame routines are discussed further in Chapter 4.

There are many other things that sap our energy as well. Any form of family stress can cause fatigue on the field or court. Home should be a place that is soothing to a competitor, a place where they make deposits to their energy stores rather than withdrawals. If home is not a safe place, it can cause tremendous harm not only to energy levels but also to overall psychological functioning. This is one of the reasons that when children are abused in their homes they tend to have emotional problems that need to be addressed. If home is unsafe, then it can feel like the world as a whole is unsafe. If there are problems in your home, they are likely affecting your ability to excel athletically, whether you realize it or not. Address these issues. Seek help when the situation warrants it.

Energy depletion from family concerns extends to significant others as well. Blocking out a fight with your girlfriend or boyfriend while competing is extremely challenging. Even if you are skilled enough to be able to block these problems out, they are likely affecting you even if not on a conscious level. In the case of Luke, Lindsay, and the rest of the track team, this truth annihilated their psychic and physical energy levels.

Work can also be a significant detractor from your "get up and go." When one is completely drained physically, it is very hard to sit and focus on paperwork or studying. It is in this way that physical and mental energy are linked. The best way to address this issue is to manage your time well. If you are the type to procrastinate with work, then it will end up weighing on you. Get it done early and it can even energize you just to know that your work is completed.

The take-home message in this chapter is to plan and be smart with how you manage your life and energy stores. One simple example is strategizing about mornings. Starting out your day under stress sets you up for failure and fatigue at all of the wrong times. First, do not hit your snooze button excessively. Doing so interferes with your normal sleep/wake patterns and can lead to daytime drowsiness. Another major mistake is having caffeine immediately after waking up in the morning. Our bodies naturally produce chemicals that wake us up in the morning. Adding caffeine to the mix often creates a rush of energy that leaves quickly and causes you to crash later. Wait a while after waking up before having that cup of coffee.

Stress equals energy loss. Are you usually hurrying in the morning? Do you normally run late? Nothing can be more stressful than knowing you will be late to work, class, practice, or a team bus. Complete as many tasks as possible before the morning arrives. Shower at night rather than in the morning. Do not expect yourself to be able to pack the morning of a team trip. Do not drink heavily the night before an early morning. If you tend to run late, wake up 15 minutes earlier than you generally would. The loss of 15 minutes of sleep is easily justified in the context of maintaining your sanity and arriving on time. In this case, 15 minutes less sleep will likely give you more energy in the end by lowering stress.

Another method for saving your power for more important things is to put seemingly unimportant decisions on cruise control. For example, if your team can commit to all wearing the same T-shirt and shorts to a team lifting session, it will save the minor stress of having to choose an outfit. The minor amount of stress that this saves across an entire team adds up to something more significant. Routines are important here. On average, athletes who are prone to routine tend to do better than those that are not. Taking this a step further, if your team can set a specific outfit for every day of the week, you are adding up even more energy saved.

Nutrition is also key here. Not only is good nutrition important to your physical strength and muscle growth, but it is also needed for your mental energy. The best way to demonstrate this is by looking at the way that many psychiatric medications such as antidepressants work. Think of your brain as a series of rooms. The rooms have to be able to communicate with each other, but often the doors are closed, which makes communications difficult or impossible. When these doors are sealed shut, depression can occur because the parts of our brains that need to speak to each other are unable to do so through locked doors. Antidepressants serve as the keys to open the doors (incidentally, talk therapy and exercise can also open these doors). However, the good nutrition that we get is the actual communication between the rooms. You can think of that chicken salad you eat as making your brain cells work properly. Without proper nutrition, talk therapy, exercise, and antidepressants cannot fix the problem.

You can also manage energy intelligently by making smart decisions. Do you need to get to the mall to return or buy something? Think about when you want to do it. Maybe you can do it at 10 a.m. and work out later. Alternatively, you can work out at 10 a.m. and go to the mall later in the day. The right answer in this scenario is to get to the mall earlier. If you can avoid crowds, you can save yourself the stress of being unable to find a parking spot and having to wait on long lines.

Preserving and improving energy levels in game is also key. Think of the catcher who has to constantly communicate with the other eight players on her softball team. It is frequently her job along with coaches to tell the team where to align themselves for each batter. Communicating with the outfielders can be a major drain, especially when playing in a doubleheader. Rather than screaming, think about how else you might be able to relay messages to outfielders. Can you whistle loudly to get their attention? Are you able to communicate your commands through hand signals? If you can, you will thank yourself in the 7th inning of Game 2 that day.

Helping others is important. A major challenge that team leaders face is knowing the line between how much to help others and how much to focus on oneself. It is important to be selfish to an extent so as to sustain energy. However, I am a firm believer that teaching others reinforces important skills. Some people even find that helping others is a great way to feel positive about oneself and reenergize.

What about after games and during free time? This is a great time to make deposits into the energy bank. In this age of smartphones it can be very difficult to be fully mindful and focus on restoring energy. It is also quite difficult because of the increasing demands on our time. What I challenge many of my athletes to do when they are too busy is to schedule time for relaxation and manage it intelligently. If you don't take this approach, then you probably will not have time for mindful relaxation. My idea of relaxation for an athlete is to start by texting anyone who will try to get in touch with you that you'll be unavailable for 22 minutes. Then, take your phone, put it on silent, and turn it upside down. Watch any Netflix show for 22 minutes. This is a terrific way to force yourself into relaxation and rebuild psychic energy.

What is even better, if possible, is to mindfully watch the sport that you love on TV. Are you a baseball player? I challenge you to turn your phone over and watch a 3-hour baseball game. Can you even imagine doing that—sitting in one place for 3 hours without constantly tweeting, snapchatting, texting, or emailing? This is an even better way to replenish your mental energy.

Deeper into Maintaining Energy

Depending on how serious you are about your career in athletics, you should be working closely with a nutritionist and a strength coach to better understand exactly how food and exercise affect your energy. There is a reason that athletes today are bigger and faster than they were years ago. There is a reason that Olympic records continue to be broken year after year. Science is advancing. Everyone is looking to gain an edge. Nutrition and exercise are huge ones. If you are not taking advantage of the developments in science in these areas, the person next to you certainly is, and they'll be happy to take your spot.

As a high school, college, or professional athlete, you have enough on your plate. No matter how much you learn on the internet about the foods you eat, that does not make you a dietician. No matter how much you learn about muscle growth, that does not certify you as a strength coach. Think of a football team that is threatening to score a touchdown in the red area and the quarterback throws a pick-six (an interception for a touchdown the other way). This is a 14-point swing. A positive becomes a major negative. Diet and exercise work the same way. If you try to manage it yourself and make mistakes, you are essentially throwing a pick-six. You think that you're making a major gain, but you are setting yourself back. You cannot be an expert in all things. Trust those who are. That does not mean that you can't question the experts. It just means that you need their understanding of the science to push you forward and maximize your energy levels.

In addition to all of the aforementioned techniques, it is crucial to manage your emotions to your advantage. Anger can be a good thing. Yes, I'll say it again: anger can be a useful emotion. Anger is often the easiest emotion to use to replace another negative emotion. That's why men and women often find reasons to get angry at their exes after they break up. Anger can be useful in overcoming feelings of sadness that seem insurmountable. However, this is only true for people who can control their anger. Any person who has a history of violence or fighting should work more toward moving away from anger rather than making use of it. Anger is a powerful and useful emotion, but only when controlled.

Anger can also be helpful when athletes need an edge. In long playoff series it's common for players (and even fans) to find someone on the opposing team to get mad at. Maybe it was a hard foul that triggered the anger. Maybe it was some trash-talking that got under your skin. Here, too, anger can be helpful when it is controlled. Controlled anger can push you harder. Uncontrolled anger can lead you to become sloppy, unfocused, or even fight. It is an emotion that gives as readily as it takes away.

Anger also can have severe consequences for your energy stores. Ask yourself the question: is my anger becoming "hate"? Do I hate the person that I'm playing against? If you do, then you have lost control and are draining your power bank. Anger and hate can consume people. If you find yourself struggling with anger and hate, then it's time to refocus. Get your mind back onto what matters. For more help in this area see Chapter 3, "Own Your Thoughts."

Floyd Mayweather

Outside the ring, it would seem that Floyd Mayweather would be incapable of having the approach necessary to preserve energy to his advantage. He has made many questionable decisions in his personal life. However, he is regarded by many as being one of the greatest boxers of all time. This is not because he is necessarily the strongest or fastest fighter.

What Mayweather does better than almost anyone else in boxing is to plan, box defensively, and preserve his energy. When in the ring, he makes it look like there is no wasted motion. If he sways, it is to realistically fool his opponent. If he ducks, it is in order to dodge an actual punch. If he throws a punch, it is because he can realistically land it. There is no wasted energy, no unnecessary

© Getty Images

moving parts. It is for this reason that opponents often do not stand a chance if they go the distance with him. By the time he gets to the end of the fight, he will have expended less energy than you. Subsequently, his punches will be stronger and his movements will be more purposeful. Additionally, because he typically maintains more energy in reserve, he is exceedingly difficult to knock down.

3   Own Your Thoughts (Focus)

Gina has always been a ferocious competitor. For as long as she could remember, all she ever wanted was to play for the US national softball team someday. Her father, a former minor league baseball player, had always been very supportive of her dreams. He worried that she only pursued softball because of his passion for baseball. His concern was that she was just trying to make him happy. He was supportive of her dreams, but would never force her if she lost interest. For Gina, losing interest was never an issue. She started with T-ball at the age of 3 and her love for both baseball and softball developed from there. Having been raised in Texas, she had the benefit of playing her sport year-round in at least reasonably warm weather.

In the few weeks between seasons, her father would pitch to her in their sprawling backyard. He trained her to hit from both sides of the plate, as he felt it would help develop her offensive game more thoroughly. Gina also had a love of professional baseball and watched games whenever she could.

If ever there was a criticism of Gina as a ballplayer, it was that she never had to struggle and overcome adversity. She lived in a loving home with her father, mother, and older brother (a football player). She had a knowledgeable and sensitive father coaching her. Her family was comfortable financially and could afford to provide her with the right equipment, mentors, and tutors so that she could keep up academically.

Gina got used to being the best player on her team. At every level she dominated. She pitched, played first base, and hit as well as any teammate. She won championships at the high school and Amateur Athletic Union (AAU) levels along with countless awards and accolades. Eventually, letters came pouring in from Power Five schools desperate to sign her up. The day she signed her letter of intent to play in the Southeastern Conference (SEC) was the happiest of her life. Her dream of playing for the national team was within view. She spent the summer training harder than ever.

When she arrived on campus in August, Gina did not think she would be great; she knew it. Fall softball (the non-championship season with exhibition scrimmages) went exactly as planned. She pitched, hit, and played defense precisely as she had expected. She won the love and support of her teammates and coaches quickly as she eagerly awaited the spring championship season.

When the first pitch finally came, Gina got the nod as a freshman starting at first base, a very high honor. She did not disappoint, going 2 for 3 and playing solidly in the field in her team's first win of the year. It was all turning out exactly as she had planned. The next day, in a doubleheader, she started again. The first game did not go as well, with her going hitless. In the second game of the day she went hitless again, making two errors. Her struggles continued from there before she found herself stuck in the worst slump of her career. For the first time in her softball life, Gina wondered if she belonged. Soon she lost her starting position.

In her occasional pinch-hitting appearances, she found her mind racing. It seemed that she was thinking about ten different stressful thoughts all at once. "What if I strike out again?" "Can I hit this pitcher?" "Will I lose my scholarship?" "Am I standing in the right area of the batter's box?" "Can I time her pitches?".

Many people are surprised to hear me tell them that our minds are only capable of holding one thought at a time. They might tell me: "Dr. Wald, I have ten things running through my mind right now." In fact, what that person is doing is cycling through thoughts. It seems that they are focused on ten things at the same time, but what is really happening is they are rapidly moving from one thought to another and another. If we could freeze time and gain insight into a person's active thoughts at a given moment, we would find only one thought present. This may seem like a trivial distinction, but it is crucial in maintaining performance at the highest levels.

This concept is the very basis of meditation and hypnosis. Meditation and hypnosis involve taking a thought and having it remain at the front of a person's mind for as long as he or she chooses. This process can be guided or self-directed. Most people have been in a state of hypnosis of sorts even if they have not realized it. Have you ever been driving on the highway and listening to a song or thinking about something that happened at work and driven right past your exit? In that moment, you were in a state of hypnosis. You were focused on something to the exclusion of everything else in your environment. If this has happened to you, it is a very positive sign. It means that you are indeed capable of focusing on something for an extended period to the exclusion of everything else in your environment.

You may be asking, what is the benefit of focusing on one thought? The answer is simply that for every moment that you are in control of your thoughts, you are not thinking about issues that are unhelpful to your progress as an athlete. This simple process can create relaxation and a positive sense of well-being. It may seem overly simplistic. However, the hard part is keeping that thought in your mind when another stressful thought is trying to intrude and take over your mind space. When one is struggling and beginning the process of learning to "own their thoughts," it is a good idea to pay attention to how long one can go without reverting to thinking about the problematic issue. The more stressful the situation, the harder it can be to take control of your mind space. For a person who is a true "worrier," this may mean controlling their thoughts for 3 or 5 seconds at a time before other thoughts take over again. However, each one of those seconds is a victory. This process is like building a muscle. It takes time, repetition, and persistence, but the ability to control what you think about at any given moment is invaluable in sport.

Why are some athletes "clutch" while others seem to fall apart in big moments? It comes down to maintaining composure and concentration on your swing thought, or pitch thought, or free throw thought, or pre-race thought. The non-clutch athlete will lose focus and think about the outcome of his at bat or free throw. What if I hit this shot? What if I miss it? Will this loss be my fault? Anything that takes you away from your one thought is a detriment to your success. By contrast, the clutch athlete is in control of the thought at the front of their mind. They do not think: if I sink this putt, I win the tournament. They treat the putt as they would any other. Whether it is on the 1st, 3rd, or 18th green, it is all the same.

This then begs the question: what should I think about? This will be different for each person. The free throw in basketball is a very common place for a player to get the yips. It should be easy. No one is trying to block your shot! Just hit the free throw! The player who struggles with free throws often allows unhelpful thoughts to enter and create anxiety. Why can't I do this? Are people going to think there's something wrong with me if my field goal percentage is higher than my free throw percentage?

If you are a long-time basketball player, you have shot free throws thousands of times. The motion of making a proper free throw is etched in your mind. It is as easy as walking. For this type of problem, the fix is often to allow a relaxing thought to take over while your body does the work of shooting on its own. If you can think about a loved one who makes you happy or a vacation from your youth, the work of hitting the free throw will happen on its own. This is the most effective method to deal with the old cliché of "overthinking it."

Everyone is different. For other competitors, the thought will be more beneficial if it is directly related to your sport. When a golfer begins to slump, various thoughts often start to take over. As a sport psychologist, I am very much opposed to golfers having multiple swing thoughts as, again, there is only room for one thought at a time. This can only confuse the issue. The golf swing, much like the previously mentioned free throw, is ingrained in your muscle memory. It is almost never a good idea to tinker with your swing dramatically in the middle of a match. Let your swing take over.

For some golfers, the swing thought will be one problem that they frequently have with their swing. In those cases, the thought might be "straighten the elbow, straighten the elbow, straighten the elbow." If a golfer is extremely comfortable with their swing, the thought may be as simple as "ball, ball, ball."

Think about it. Sports are simple! Hit a ball with a bat, put a ball through a hoop, shoot a puck in a goal. We as flawed human beings complicate things and become our own worst enemies. Make the sport simple again. One thought. One goal.

Where does this leave Gina? Gina's struggles were particularly challenging as she had never failed in softball in any significant way. Because she was so successful in the past, she never had to make real use of many mental skills. Sports came easily to her in the past. She practiced, she showed up, and she dominated.

The problem for Gina was that the stakes had been raised. The competition was greater than it ever had been before, forcing Gina to develop mentally as opposed to only physically. Slowly, in time, Gina would stop before she entered the batter's box and focus on the center field wall, only for a second. This was a reminder that it was time for her to go into her "hypnotic state" and focus on one idea to the exclusion of everything else in the world.

Gina had enough confidence in her swing that she wanted to leave it as is. Through years and years of training, she felt she had developed it properly. She let her swing take care of itself and focused on the big yellow softball and nothing else. Much like the aforementioned golfer, her thought became "ball, ball, ball." She developed to a point where her mind perceived that there was no crowd and no fielders around her. All she could see was the ball.

It is important to note here that Gina's focus was what we would refer to as an external focus. In other words, she was keeping her mind on something outside her mind: the ball. However, internal focus, or thoughts about something inside the mind, work better for some. An internal thought might be something like "relax, relax, relax." This is where you as the athlete get to create your own unique style. Experiment and figure out what works best for you.

Imagery

A common theme you may notice in this book is how talented athletes can get by on raw ability at lower levels, but must find new skills if they wish to advance once the stakes are raised. Imagine Tyra, the 6'3" center from Texas. In high school it seemed like there was no competition for her. Sure, she was playing at the highest levels in the high school system in the state of Texas, but her height gave her an advantage in both rebounding and scoring that was unmatched. Leading her team to wins was possible whether she practiced hard or not. She seemed to be equally effective regardless of her preparation.

However, as is almost always the case, Division 1 college basketball provided a surprisingly difficult challenge for this high school standout. Height did not give her an insurmountable advantage. Other girls were tall as well. The ones who weren't as tall seemed to have athleticism that allowed them to compete with her for rebounds. Even the shorter players found ways to contest her shots. At times, she felt like her height was a liability, as it seemed like she was always the last one down the floor in transition. Upon entering college, not only was it crucial for Tyra to take her physical preparation more seriously, but she also had to take her mental training more seriously. She found that imagery made a tremendous difference in her confidence and overall performance.

One of the most commonly used tools of sport psychologists is imagery. When people take the time to see themselves succeeding in their own minds before they take the court, they are better prepared to make the vision a reality. For some, this process comes naturally. For others, it feels like being a fish swimming upstream.

What is most important in this process is knowing that no one is perfect at making use of imagery. There is also a wide range of what could be considered effective imagery usage. It can happen with eyes open or closed. It can be as quick as 30 seconds or it can last hours. It can include a great deal of detail or it can focus on only the most important aspect of success.

One effective method of inducing a state of mental preparedness for imagery utilization is by beginning with an exercise such as progressive muscle relaxation (PMR). Incidentally, PMR is also very effective for general relaxation and management of stress. Here, again, as long as one gets the nuts and bolts of the process, there is no wrong way to do it.

The way that I like to use PMR is as follows. Find a quiet, relatively dark location. Get into a comfortable seated or lying position and close your eyes. Start by tensing the muscles in your toes, feet, calves, thighs, and butt. Clench those muscles so much that it almost hurts (of course, if you have a medical condition that makes this process too painful or dangerous, do not practice PMR). Focus on that pain and discomfort to the exclusion of everything else in the world. Imagine that pain having physical properties like a cloud of smoke. Maybe it has a color. Maybe it is green or red—any color you choose. Imagine that pain and discomfort, with all of its tangible properties, entering the lower half of your body. See it settling in your legs and feet. All the while, breathe slowly all the way into your gut and all the way out. There is no right amount of time to allow this discomfort to sit in your lower body. Whatever you can tolerate is the right amount for you. Maybe it is 10 seconds, and maybe it is 2 minutes.

Next, imagine all of that discomfort with all of its physical properties leaving your body. See it float away and dissipate. While this is happening, relax your toes, your feet, your calves, your thighs, and your butt. Meanwhile, still breathe all the way into your gut and all the way out. Notice how, for some strange reason, you feel very relaxed. Spend the next minute or so breathing all the way in and all the way out.

Next, imagine that discomfort returning with all of its physical properties. As you see it, clench your fists, arms, and jaw. See that discomfort entering the upper half of your body. All the while, breathe all the way in and all the way out. Notice how it seems that there is nothing in the world other than that pain as you see it in your body. Hold that pain inside yourself for whatever amount of time feels right for you.

Next, imagine that pain and all its physical properties leaving you. See that colored cloud float away and dissipate as you relax your hands, arms, and jaw. All the while, breathe all the way in and all the way out. Again, for some strange reason, you feel very relaxed. Remain in this relaxed state for whatever amount of time feels right for you.

One of the most important benefits of PMR for our purposes, in addition to general relaxation, is to get your mind into the state where you are focused fully on one thought to the exclusion of everything else in the world. Once your mind has had time to enter this hypnotic/meditative state, you can now focus our attention on visualizing success. After the PMR exercise is complete, keep your eyes closed and imagine the venue you are about to compete in. If it is a basketball game, see the court clearly in your mind. Is there a logo on the court? What does the court feel like beneath your sneakers? What do your uniforms look like? What do your opponent's uniforms look like? See every detail as if it is really happening.

Now that you are present in the moment, see yourself on that court, in the game, carrying out the role that is uniquely yours. If you are a point guard, see yourself bringing the ball up from the backcourt. Notice how clear the floor looks to you, and how easy it is to spot your open teammate under the basket. Appreciate how your court vision has never been more crystal clear.

Owning Your Thoughts and Sleep

On a somewhat related note, the PMR technique described in detail in this chapter can be related to difficulty with sleep. Insomnia is an extremely common problem that destroys athletic performance. Sleep becomes even harder to get with the stresses of being a student athlete or the frustration of a slump. The way that I like to describe it, falling asleep requires two processes: keeping the mind free of stress and relaxing the body.

Keeping the mind free of stress is very similar to owning your thoughts. If the stresses in your life are dominating your mind space, then it will be extremely difficult to fall asleep. You cannot fix your problems while trying to fall asleep in bed, so you might as well relax! While trying to sleep, it is important to focus your mind on less stressful issues, as has been discussed throughout this chapter. However, if this proves to be too difficult, reading a book is the next best thing. If you are focused on your taxes, your boss, or a fight you had with your friend, then your chances of falling asleep are very low!

Relaxing the body is also crucial for people who suffer from insomnia. It is important to find a position in bed that allows every muscle in your body to rest. If your neck or shoulders are tensed, then it will be that much more difficult to fall asleep. What I feel is most important is focusing on the hands, the shoulders, and breathing. Often, people in bed will fidget with their hands or shrug their shoulders. If you notice yourself doing either of these, that is a good sign that your body is not relaxed. Also, deep breathing is one of the most effective ways to slow our nervous systems down. While in bed, your breaths should be slow and go deep into the belly.

One important thing to note is that every time you shift positions, you must begin the process of relaxing your body all over again. Try to find a position that you are comfortable in, one that you are likely to fall asleep in, and stick to it. If you experience minor discomfort, try to stay put. Obviously, if you are very uncomfortable you should move. However, just keep in mind that continuously tossing and turning just pushes sleep further and further away.

Experts in sleep also use a number of excellent suggestions that have been shown to help people who struggle with sleep. First, your sleep environment should be cool, quiet, and dark. This is a good place to add that those bright red numbers staring you in the face on your alarm clock are probably not helping! Consider covering them. Sleep experts also encourage us to use our beds only for sex and sleep. That means if you have difficulty falling or staying asleep, you should not eat, watch television, or do work in bed. Other tips include getting out of bed if you are unable to sleep for an extended period and beginning the process of relaxing and getting ready for bed up to 2 hours before it is time to go to sleep.

Some people would say that using the technique of owning your thoughts is simply a method of distraction and does not force a person to deal with underlying issues in a real way. I completely agree with that view! The technique of owning one's thoughts should be used in conjunction with the other techniques described in this book so as to allow one to truly overcome their troubles. However, the ability to be in control of one's thoughts is a very important skill for maintaining emotional stability.

Executive Functioning

When discussing focus, it is important to bring up the overarching topic of executive functioning. Executive functioning can be defined in many ways. It is the term that is used to define those cognitive abilities (thinking skills) that are managed by the frontal lobe of our brain. Another way to define executive functioning is as an umbrella term for all of those cognitive functions related to controlling one's thoughts and behaviors. Take a minute to think about all of the different activities that we do in order to manage our behavior and thoughts. Executive functioning includes our concentration, longer term attention, working memory, ability to shift our mindset from one idea to another, ability to control our emotions, and ability to organize and plan.

If a person suffers a brain injury, they can lose the ability to manage any of these abilities. Losing one executive function may not seem like a big deal. given that there are several others, but think about each individual ability in isolation. Losing the ability to plan and organize could leave a person unable to even use a piece of paper properly. A person with difficulty in this area might forget how to use an entire piece of paper when writing and end up almost putting thoughts down on the desk holding the piece of paper. Deficiencies in this area can also leave a person unable to keep on topic when speaking because of an inability to properly order their thoughts. These abilities all fall under the category of executive functioning.

In fact, in order to compete in athletics at an elite level, one's executive functioning skills have to be working in concert almost perfectly. Earlier, the idea of working memory was mentioned. This is the ability to take in information, juggle it around in your head, and use the juggled information to make sense of what you are doing. Think of a quarterback going through progressions. As they look out into an ocean of 21 other bodies scattered around them, they have to see who is an eligible receiver. Then they have to see if an eligible receiver is open. Then they must move on to the next receiver if the first one is not open. Once all of this has registered in the mind of the quarterback, only then can the physical skills and abilities take over with a strong, accurate throw. An inability to juggle any of this information well in a few short seconds leaves a quarterback vulnerable and ineffective.

The quarterback who has difficulty with this type of multitasking and shifting of mindset has to start by slowing things down. If you can't go through this process effectively at full speed, try doing it at half speed. If you don't have teammates and coaches who can help you with this, then close your eyes and visualize it. Go through the process in your mind repeatedly and make each repetition slightly faster than the previous one.

Think next about the ice hockey goalie's ability to concentrate for a fraction of a second. If the frontal lobe of the goalie does not perform this function flawlessly, it renders him or her ineffective. The goalie generally has fractions of a second to lock in and concentrate on a tiny black puck in order to get in front of it. If concentration is lost for even a hundredth of a second, then they likely will be looking at a red light flashing behind them.

Let's put this all together so that we can demonstrate just how immaculately a person's executive functioning skills must work in order to compete at the highest levels. Think about the beach volleyball player diving to dig a ball that is likely to land just in bounds. First, the player has to lock in and concentrate on the ball. If this concentration is lost for a fraction of a second, tracking the ball becomes almost impossible. Next, he or she must mentally manipulate the boundaries of the court against the ball in order to predict if the ball is going to land in bounds or out of bounds. A failure here can cost a point if the ball was going to land out of bounds and was misperceived as being in bounds. This takes a lot of skill in planning and organizing visual information. The volleyball player will also have to shift his or her gaze back and forth from the ball to the boundary line in order to make a decision about whether or not to follow through on the dig.

Here, if all of the components of executive functioning are not working in harmony, then there is no hope of salvaging the point. To take it a step beyond just this play, emotional control is also an important executive function as mentioned. Players who lack this skill tend to yell at teammates when frustrated. Mistreat enough people this way and you will quickly find yourself without a team.

In this chapter we have discussed the concept of focusing on one idea or object to the exclusion of everything else. However, using this type of focus is not the only way to prepare your executive functioning skills to work optimally.

Many athletes tell me that their focus will naturally go into the optimal place as long as their minds "go blank." In other words, as long as a person doesn't get "stuck inside their own head," then the ideal state of mind comes to them without any further effort (such as actively focusing on one object or idea to the exclusion of all others). For this type of athlete the best approach is to become adept at clearing the mind of negative or unhelpful thoughts rather than actively focusing on one. Unhelpful thoughts can include negative self-talk relating to others, such as "That guy is way better than me." It can also include unhelpful ideas like "My mechanics are all messed up." For the athlete who functions best through the "going blank" method, almost any non-negative thought can work. Notice that I said "non-negative" and not "positive." This is because even neutral thoughts like "This course is kept really well" can work. This certainly also includes positive self-talk such as "I'm hitting my driver really well today." This method does not work for everybody. In fact, in my experience, I would say that more athletes do best with an active and beneficial thought. The point here is that there is more than one way to optimize one's thought process and executive functioning for athletic success.

Evan Longoria

Having worked with the great mental skills expert and kinesiology professor Ken Ravizza, Evan Longoria learned the value of experts in sport psychology. He has been open about the benefit he has gotten from focusing on mental skills. Longoria has gotten into the habit of using the top of the left foul pole as a point to focus on before at bats and whenever he needs to regroup following a mistake. In a sense, this is a method of forcing himself to own his thoughts, focus on one thing to the exclusion of other distractions, and set himself up for success.

4 Curb Your Enthusiasm (Pre-performance Routines and Focus)

Dara grew up in New York City and she loved the energy that she felt in its streets. From the age of 5 she remembers wondering why anyone would ever want to live anywhere else. In the city, she had everything a person could need. This included her favorite restaurant (a pizza place around the corner from her Upper West Side home), all of her friends within a 20-block radius (about 1 square mile), and most importantly for her, Central Park.

Dara's mother had always been a major tennis enthusiast, having earned a position on a college tennis team when she was younger. From the time she was a child, Dara wanted to emulate her mother in every way. Living near to Central Park was important to both of them because it gave them access to the outdoors and tennis. Young Dara took lessons in Central Park almost as soon as she could walk. Her mother also supplemented her lessons by playing with her as often as she could.

As a little girl, Dara always seemed to have too much energy, which made raising her in a small two-bedroom apartment challenging for her parents. As she got older, she became obsessed with her tennis rankings within the state of New York. This made her intensely competitive and desperate to win. Before matches, she seemed to be bouncing off the walls to let out her overflowing energy.

Despite her enthusiasm for the game, Dara seemed to plateau. Her play in matches always seemed to be subpar relative to her overall skill as a tennis player. She won few tournaments and could never compete with the best players in her age group.

Contrasting Styles

In contrast to Dara, Jean was a calm, collected young man who excelled in school. Growing up in Alberta, Canada, hockey was everything. Jean watched every Calgary Flames game, refusing to spend time away from the TV during games. If it was absolutely necessary for him to be away, the game was taped.

It was understood that you did not tell Jean the final score of the games before he watched the whole thing.

Jean's favorite player had always been Jarome Iginla. He admired the way Iginla played the game in a tough, rugged way while also being an elite scorer. When his favorite player was traded away, Jean was devastated. However, he committed himself to continuing to follow Iginla's career and fashioning his own game after him.

Before his games, Jean would sit in his tiny locker in the freezing locker room where his team of 12-year-olds played their home games. He seemed to be in almost a trance-like state, visualizing himself making plays that he had seen Iginla make. He prided himself on strong back-checking in the defensive zone and mastery of deflecting shots from the point in the offensive zone. While he was one of the best in his league, he seemed to start games slowly. When looking over his stats (which he kept track of himself), he saw that he scored few goals in the first period, somewhat more in the second, and the majority in the third.

Pregame Routines

Pregame routines are a more serious issue than many people think they are. Poor pregame routines can negatively affect performance over the course of an entire game. The traditional way of looking at pregame levels of energy/arousal is that a person should find a balance between being overly energetic and overly calm. Many mental skills professionals believe that moderate arousal is perfect. However, I believe that this issue is extremely dynamic and should vary depending on a number of factors including personal preference, the sport being played, general personality factors, and past performances. Most golfers are not well served to be slamming their bodies into their lockers and slapping their teammates in the side of the head before matches. This further illustrates that each situation is unique and requires a specific plan with regard to pregame.

Football is an interesting example of the complexity of pregame routines. Enter a locker room 30 minutes before a team takes the field and you may find that the players remaining in the locker room are lying back in their lockers quietly listening to music on their headphones. If you enter that same locker 30 seconds before the team takes the field, you would be more likely to see players jumping up and down, screaming, and yelling.

Every person has to find their own level of pregame energy based on all of the aforementioned factors. Self-monitoring is important in this process. Ask yourself after a game: am I happy with my effort today? What was I doing before the game? Was I calm and focused? Was I hyped? Was I somewhere in between? These are important questions to answer if you are looking to get the most out of yourself.

Going back to our two athletes and their pregame routines, they probably would have been better off completely swapping the way they approached their sports in relation to their personalities. Dara is overly energetic naturally and plays a sport that requires extremely long periods of intense focus on a small yellow ball. Meanwhile, Jean is generally calm and focused playing a sport involving high-speed collisions and a very rapid pace of play. Dara is an athlete who needs to calm and focus herself. Jean is an athlete who is needs to hype himself up. Ask yourself: what is my general level of arousal as a person overall? Am I playing a sport that rewards focus more or energy more? How do I balance the two so that I can have as much of both as possible? Tailor your pregame energy around your needs. This will put you in the best possible position to succeed.

Pre–at Bat vs. Pregame Routines

When not managed properly, excessive energy can cost a player their focus. The goal is not to have a sloppy unfocused type of surge. We want a deadly, focused sort of an energy. When you look at the recent history of baseball, steroids have become a major topic of conversation. Steroids help players gain muscle mass and, almost as importantly, they help players heal and recover quickly. This makes them beneficial even to pitchers who are often worn down the day after an outing. It goes without saying that the use of steroids comes with a high price.

Other drugs, however, have been abused more rampantly throughout the history of baseball. Cocaine and other amphetamines can provide a boost in energy and focus, both of which are crucial in baseball. Ultimately, a baseball player without some level of focus is ineffective. Imagine a great outfielder, maybe Ken Griffey Jr., running back on a fly ball, digging a cleat into the wall, reaching over the fence, and pulling back a home run—an incredible feat, likely to make the SportsCenter Top 10. Sure, Ken Griffey Jr. in his day was faster and more athletic than almost anyone else, but there are other factors that make players like him great.

There are countless minor league and college ballplayers who have incredible speed and agility. There are also countless minor league and college players who have the agility and athleticism to dig a cleat into the wall, reach over a fence, and pull a home run away just like Griffey. So what is the greatest factor that separates a player like Ken Griffey Jr. from the rest? It is the ability to do all of those physical feats at full force while tracking the flight of a 375-foot fly ball. His ability to do all of these actions simultaneously and with great focus is what makes him an all-time great.

The same idea holds true in other sports. Odell Beckham Jr. has made incredible one-handed catches throughout his career. Any football fan remembers his one-handed touchdown catch while falling over backwards against the Dallas Cowboys. However, I have seen many incredibly athletic receivers who have the capacity to make astonishing one-handed catches. These are also players with immense speed and agility. Here, just like with Ken Griffey Jr., what makes Odell Beckham Jr. great is his ability to run at full speed, reach back with one hand, and make an incredible catch, all while tracking a football over a 50-yard throw.

Deadly focus is in my opinion what separates the boys from the men in sports. Mind you, focus is a complex topic. It does not just include the ability to stare at an object and track its flight. It also requires immense skill in multi-tasking. Imagine all of the thoughts that Beckham kept in mind while making his catch. Tracking the flight of the ball, knowing where he was on the field so as not to go out of bounds, knowing where the defender was, maintaining his balance, and manipulating his body were all thoughts that went through his mind over those brief few seconds. His mind also had to shift back and forth rapidly between these factors. He may have thought about each one for a fraction of a second several times during that play. He likely shifted back and forth between the above thoughts several times. Ask yourself the question: is that something I can do? Remember, once you get to the elite levels, sports can be cruel. If this is not a skill that you can develop at least to a certain extent, then you won't make it.

Returning to the idea of pregame rituals versus pre–at bat routines, there is an important distinction that we must draw. With pregame routines, you can be more amped up or more relaxed. You can jump up and down and yell or you can take a nap, depending on your sport and personality style. However, when you step into the on-deck circle, there can be a wrong way to work. You need to harness as much focus as possible while maintaining an effective energy level. There is a balance. If you are not spending time in the dugout and in the on-deck circle tracking pitches and getting yourself into the right frame of mind, you are lowering your own chances of reaching base safely.

There is no one pre–at bat routine that is right for everyone. One example of a pre–at bat routine might involve tracking all pitches closely while in the dug-out, using a weighted bat to stretch and time the pitcher while in the on-deck circle, and then calming one's breathing while walking to the batter's box. In between pitches it may be helpful to refocus your eyes on the ball. If it is in the pitcher's glove, then focus on the glove.

There is also no one pregame routine that is right for everyone. One example of a pregame baseball routine might involve 5 minutes of PMR (discussed in Chapter 3), 5 minutes in the batting cage, and 10 minutes of fielding practice followed by going through all of the regular team routines and batting practice. These amounts of time may be far too long or short for some. This can be figured out best through a process of trial and error.

Post–at Bat

There is a cost to being overly energized and uncontrolled both before and after your at bat. Ask yourself: what do I usually do when I strike out? Do I curse? Do I slam my bat? What about when I go 0 for 4 in a game? Does my bad game carry over into the next day? A great way to go into a prolonged slump is to carry bad at bats from yesterday into today. Struggling in any area of sports can produce anxiety when you have high aspirations or when you are trying to hold on to your job. The competitors that are best equipped to have shorter slumps are the ones who remain even-keeled even when they are performing poorly. You should never be the player teammates stay away from after you strike out for fear of getting hit with a flying bat. Just because a big leaguer acts that way does not make it right. It just means that they could be even better than they already are if they could manage their emotions better.

Take a big picture look at your season. Know that you will have struggles at times throughout the year. When they come, remember that there is a law of averages. You will not go 4 for 4 every day. The most important point here is that the great athletes are not the ones who do not struggle; they are the ones who shorten the length of time that their struggles last by maintaining perspective on the bigger picture.

Superstition vs. Routine

Many of the greatest athletes of all time have had superstitions. Patrick Roy was very superstitious. He made it a point never to skate on top of lines on the ice. Rather, he would step over them in order to avoid making contact. His longtime rival on the Boston Bruins, Ray Bourque, had a strange ritual of hitting his goalie's pads over and over again in a very specific order. Roy is one of the greatest goaltenders of all time, and Bourque is one of the greatest defensemen of all time. Were they great because they were superstitious? I find it highly unlikely that they both would not have been among the all-time greats had they not believed in superstition. However, that doesn't mean that superstition did not play any role in their success.

Being organized and having effective routines improves performance. Ask any sport psychologist and they will agree. There are a number of reasons for this. Routines provide us with comfort and in a sense remind us that no matter where we go, the sport is the same. If you can kick a ball past midfield at your home field, then you can do it on the road. A soccer goaltender getting into the habit of kicking ten balls past midfield before every game can help ground them.

In certain circumstances, routines can also help us repeat effective physical habits so that they can be done with more ease. If a golfer does not walk onto the first tee in a tournament until he successfully hits ten balls well with his driver, hits ten balls well chipping, and sinks ten putts effectively, this could be a very effective routine. Not only does it force the golfer to repeat an effective swing for the sake of muscle memory, but it also provides confidence. The question then becomes, when does a routine become a superstition? There is no reason to think that ten drives, ten chips, and ten putts is any better than 8 or 12 of the same. Is the fact that it has to be ten a superstition? Does it matter if it's a superstition rather than a routine?

In many instances with routine and superstition, the placebo effect plays a major role. The placebo effect dictates in this case that the superstition serves absolutely no purpose other than to make the athlete believe that it helped them even though it did not. As a sport psychologist, I do not in any way believe in superstitions. However, I am not necessarily against superstitions as a part of a routine. The key to differentiating between an acceptable and unacceptable superstition is the level of distress that it can cause. For our golfer mentioned above, if he gets to the course late and only has time for five drives, five chips, and five putts, will it negatively affect his performance? If it does, then we have a problem. If Patrick Roy accidentally makes contact with a blue line, will it negatively affect him? If so, then his superstition is a problem. If you have superstitions, that's fine! Just be sure that you are flexible enough to get past it if it does not happen exactly the way you want it to. If your superstition never adversely affects your performance, then it doesn't matter if it's technically a routine or a superstition.

Derek Jeter

Having grown up a Red Sox fan, no player crushed my dreams more frequently or painfully than Derek Jeter. Despite my dislike of him for this reason, I always deeply respected what he did on the baseball diamond. Jeter was extremely even-keeled, never too high and never too low. He led by example, not having to open his mouth to his teammates in order to make an emphatic statement. He also thought about the game in a manner that was beyond what most professional ballplayers can do. Recall what was perhaps his most brilliant play as a big leaguer when he flipped the ball to catcher Jorge Posada from foul territory on the first-base side of the field. Somehow, his innate baseball intelligence told him that was where he needed to be despite being so far out of position.

The most important aspect of Jeter's game that I would like my athletes to emulate, however, is his focus. If you can remember, anytime he took a pitch he stuck his head out and watched it into the catcher's mitt. It's almost a caricature of what our coaches tell us to do when they say "keep your eye on the ball." Major League Baseball is stacked with the greatest pitchers on the

© Getty Images

planet—pitchers who command the ball and can make it dance on command. If a batter follows the ball well for 55 feet and then loses track for the last 5 feet, their likelihood of hitting is near zero. High-level pitchers can start pitches in the strike zone and have them fall out at the last split-second and vice versa. Nobody understands this better than Derek Jeter. I believe that it is this level of concentration in combination with his calm demeanor that made him such a great performer in the playoffs. In the playoffs, when facing the best pitchers with the best control and movement on their pitches, he was king because of his ability to focus and remain calm. While it may not be your style to take pitches quite the same way he did, baseball players would do well to emulate his method of concentrating in the batter's box.

5   Stand Tall (Confidence)

Andy grew up in poverty in a dangerous part of town. He never met his mother or father. All he knew of them was that they struggled with drug abuse and gave him up to his mother's sister when he was a baby. His aunt cared for him as if he was her own, but she struggled to make ends meet. She also had little time for him because of her work schedule despite her best efforts. Andy tried to spend as little time as possible thinking about his parents, but he found his thoughts difficult to control. He wondered: how could someone just give me away? Was it because I was a bad baby? Is it because there is something wrong with me?

Andy did not dare share his lingering thoughts with anyone around him. Such thinking could be seen as a sign of weakness, something he could not allow to be known. Weakness often led to cruelty, bullying, and assault in his neighborhood. He put on a strong face for the outside world, although he felt insecure and broken inside.

Adding to his internal emotional struggles was Andy's academic issues. For as long as he could remember he was unable to read at the level of his class-mates. Rather than receiving the help he needed to catch up, Andy pretended not to care and fell further behind. By the time he was in the eighth grade he had been held back twice. At 13 years old, Andy was barely literate. This led to humiliation at school and only exacerbated his insecurities. He was the only one who knew his own inner thoughts. He considered himself a dumb kid who nobody wanted.

One of this young man's only positive quality in his own mind was his "tough guy" façade. He was always big and strong for his age. While he strongly dis-liked fighting, he felt that his strength was his only positive quality. He took any slight as an insult. If you bumped into Andy in the hallway, you would need to apologize quickly or suffer his wrath. There was a level of fear among even those that considered him to be a friend.

For as long as he could remember, the only thing that made Andy truly happy was football. In little league, his neighborhood had little in the way of funding to support the team. All he had known throughout his youth was old, worn-out football equipment. This included shoulder pads with mildew and helmets with insufficient padding. He also grew accustomed to playing on fields that were essentially sheets of mud with the occasional patch of grass strewn in between. None of this mattered to Andy. The football field was the one place where he was the genius. The one that was loved. The one that got people's attention for all the right reasons. This stood in stark contrast to the rest of his life where he viewed himself as worthless.

From the time he began playing, Andy dominated in every way imaginable. He played any position on both offense and defense. It always took multiple tacklers to stop him. He was superior to his peers in terms of speed, quickness, and strength. In addition to being the only place where Andy recognized his own value, the gridiron was also the only place where he gave his full effort.

Eventually, when it came time to choose a position, he settled on running back as he loved the feeling of plowing through inferior defensive players. Every team he played on focused a great deal of their offense around him. If he wasn't carrying the ball, then he was the lead blocker or major diversion for another player on his team. Amazingly, he took orders from coaches and followed the rules strictly. The fear of being kicked off of the team was always at the forefront of his mind. This fear drove him to be an excellent teammate in contrast to his behavior off the field.

Once he reached high school, Andy began getting attention from high-caliber college football programs. His confidence began to grow. He managed to get through high school by having friends do his homework. He was also able to get past any potential academic suspensions because in his town, football trumped academics.

As a result of his love of football, he was able to push himself just hard enough to get the necessary standardized test grade to be admitted to universities on an athletic scholarship. There were many red flags. Andy had gotten in trouble for fighting and cheating in the past, but college recruiters seemed to feel that with the right support system he could move past his earlier mistakes.

While he had made college campus visits, the full reality of his new life as a college student was a complete shock. Clean dorm rooms, beautiful quads of perfectly kept grass, and good food available in the cafeteria. However, the biggest shock was the quality of all things surrounding the football program. Giant lockers, brand-new high quality equipment, beautiful weight rooms, free medical care, and a giant stadium all greeted him. He was sure that having excelled with poor quality facilities and equipment in the past, he could be even more dominant with all of these new advantages.

Training camp was a rude awakening. Not only was he no longer the biggest or fastest, but his coaches yelled at him and the other players almost incessantly. He was accustomed to being the big man whose coaches had so much faith in him they didn't have to yell. He also repeatedly found himself in an unfamiliar position, on his back looking up at the sky after plays. He felt like he was average at best. As the season began, he felt fortunate not to be redshirted after such a disappointing camp.

As his struggles continued, he began having recurring thoughts about his youth and background. While there were some players on his team that had backgrounds similar to his, most came from at least middle-class homes in decent neighborhoods. Andy began to look around the locker room and feel inadequate. He attributed his struggles on the field to the fact that he just didn't belong. His mind began to bring up thoughts about how worthless he felt he was, having been left behind by his parents. He also compared himself to team-mates and how growing up in poverty made him inadequate. The worse the negative thoughts became the worse he played and vice versa.

Self-Confidence

One of the most important mental skills any competitor can have is true self-confidence. We can look at ourselves in the mirror and say we trust in ourselves, but the question will remain: do you really believe what you are saying? One of the best ways to illustrate this point is through baseball, because it is such a statistically driven sport. As a hitter stands in the batter's box, they stare at the pitcher on the mound. They may say to themselves: this is the type of pitcher that routinely strikes me out. He is a left-handed power pitcher who hides the ball well during delivery. I always have a hard time picking it up visually. In this case, if the batter is a lifetime .275 hitter, they have just dropped themselves to .250 by inserting negative thoughts in their mind. They have decreased their own chances of reaching base.

On the other hand, that same batter could stand in the batter's box and say: this is a left-handed power pitcher. It's the type of pitcher whose power I can use against him to drive the ball. He also tends to throw his fastball more frequently than most. Knowing this gives me a huge advantage. In that moment, the hitter has taken a lifetime .275 batting average and turned it into a .300 batting average just by using his mind. It all comes down to confidence. It is one thing to tell yourself you are capable, and another entirely to believe it.

The simple question then remains: how do we convince ourselves that we can accomplish what we set out to do? The most effective method is by reflecting on your own successes. The batter who raised his batting average to .300 simply called upon his past experiences in similar situations in order to give himself the necessary boost. That batter could have even gone a step further by starting in the dugout and thinking of a similar pitcher from the past who he has dominated. The more detail that the hitter can recall, the better. How tall was the pitcher? What color uniform did he wear when I faced him? What did it feel like to look at him from the batter's box?

Yet another effective method of boosting confidence is by looking at athletes that are all around and competing with you. Compare yourself to those players. This is something that athletes often do when they are frustrated over the amount of playing time they get. A volleyball player might say: I'm a much better setter than she is, but she still plays over me. This negative way of thinking can be turned into a positive if that volleyball player can use that way of thinking once she gets into the game. In such a case she might say: if she can dominate against this team, then so can I.

An important distinction should be drawn here. Comparing oneself to others that have had success is a good way to establish confidence. However, once the competition begins it is time to focus on yourself and your own performance. Comparison competition is losing competition. When golfers go out on the course, they must think only about their own performance rather than that of the golfers around them. This includes both opposing players and teammates. This also is true regardless of the format: stroke play, match play, etc. Paying attention to the leaderboard will only hinder one's ability to win. There is far too much that is outside the control of the athlete. Focusing on these variables only prevents success on the court, field, or course.

Taking this a step further, athletes who are making the most of their mental skill set should not think about winning or losing. The process of winning or losing also involves many factors that are outside the control of the competitor. For example, you may be playing against the best undiscovered talent in your conference. You cannot do anything about it other than doing your job to the best of your ability. Winning comes more easily as a by-product of focusing on oneself. It comes less easily as a result of focusing on nothing but winning. The old mantra of "do your job" rings true here.

Returning to the topic of confidence, the great majority of athletes at any level have past successes to draw from. Certainly, every athlete who has reached collegiate or professional level competition has a great deal of material to look back at. Look around you on the playing field. If you are a professional athlete, these are likely the same caliber players you faced in college or high school, just a few years later. Maybe you didn't face those actual athletes, but you likely faced highly comparable ones. If you competed against them in the past, then you can do it now.

Revisiting Andy, we see a young man who has every reason to be confident, although he is not. Certainly, there is a great deal that works against him. He did grow up with less support than most of his teammates. He also had entered a world of privilege that he was unaccustomed to.

Andy's challenge at that point was to again focus on the true reason that he and all of his teammates were there: to play football. This was not a competition in who had a larger bank account or who had a more stable family life. This was about the gridiron, a place where he always felt right. Once able to come to this realization, Andy looked around his locker room and his conference, reminding himself that this was the same sport he always dominated. They were similar opposing players that he faced, just a few years later. They were bigger and faster than in the past, but so was he. If he ruled the football field once, then he knew he would do it again. He did not think he was great, he knew it.

Preparation

Preparation is also an effective way for an athlete to feel sure of themselves as the time for competition approaches. Think of yourself when you were a student. There may have been times that you felt unprepared for an upcoming test. Maybe you did not have enough time to study. Maybe the material was difficult to grasp. That feeling of entering an exam feeling like you don't know what's coming can be pretty awful. You also probably have realized that when you go into an exam with that feeling, more often than not the test does not go well.

Alternatively, when you study intensely and walk in with confidence it can be a great feeling. You also probably have realized that when you go in with this feeling, more often than not the test does go well. This is a perfect metaphor for sports. Do you enter most games knowing what you are about to see? Are you ever surprised to see how effective an opponent is? Going into games blind is a losing strategy. It is not because of luck that baseball players tend to do better against starting pitchers the second and third time through the batting order. Once you know what's coming, you walk in with confidence.

How much tape of opponents are you watching before games? How well do you know the game plan that coach put together? Do you know all of this well enough so that there will be no major surprises on game day? Are you watching only the minimum of what your coach is requiring you to watch? Please do not expect to win unless you are willing to commit time. Excelling at high levels of athletics isn't just hard physically, it's hard mentally. It's not just physical pain you have to endure; it's mental pain. That can mean the boredom of studying a playbook again and again until you know it backwards and forwards. Your preparation is a major key to your confidence.

An example that comes to mind is a college coach who had recruited an incredibly talented group of baseball players. Winning the conference championship was expected given the level of players that had been assembled. Throughout the season, the pitching was effective, but the offense never clicked consistently. The season ended up in disappointment as they didn't even qualify for the conference tournament. After the season, the coach of the team asked me to help him figure out what had gone wrong.

After speaking to many of the players, it became clear that the team had split into two cliques. The pitchers stuck together and the position players stuck together. With the benefit of strong leadership from upperclassmen, the pitchers were constantly studying opposing batters' tendencies. They also spent a great deal of time studying tape of not only their opponents but also themselves so as to improve mechanics and to be sure they weren't tipping pitches. Meanwhile, the position players were a younger, cockier group that bought into the hype about how good they were. While they were certainly nice kids, they simply did not have anywhere near the desire to prepare as the pitchers did.

Over the course of the season, the pitchers became more and more frustrated with the position players and their unwillingness to put in the hard work necessary to help them win. As this frustration built, the wedge between the groups grew larger and larger. Lack of preparation can cost your team a season and can cost you the ability to move forward in your career.

Coaching

What I often hear from even the highest level athletes is that their coach works them too hard. On the other side, coaches seem to find themselves increasingly frustrated with the stereotypical lack of work ethic that millennials demonstrate (coaches reading this book are now nodding in agreement).

Frank Martin, head coach of the University of South Carolina men's basketball team, has responded to this issue better than anyone else I have heard. He states that the stereotypical poor work ethic that millennials demonstrate is the fault of the adults, not the kids. Kids haven't changed, the way we treat them has. In the old days a coach could frequently approach all of his players with nothing but tough love and be effective. This is no longer the case in many circumstances.

In my opinion, coaching is more challenging today than it was in the past. Coaches today must be more aware of the personalities of players they are signing or recruiting. If you as a coach do not want players with a thin skin, then do not sign or recruit them. Once they are aboard, they are indeed your responsibility. It is your responsibility to help them grow as people and to get the most out of them. In this era, some athletes will not give you the best performance and work ethic if you are overly tough on them. The question each coach must ask on a case-by-case basis is: how do I get my athlete to the point where they are strong enough emotionally that some tough love will not cause them to shut down? How do I create a strong work ethic in my athlete?

These days, you as a coach cannot be a hammer, as not all of your athletes are nails. This is true of college and professional athletes alike. One of the most important skills—if not the most important—that coaches today must possess is the ability to figure out what each player needs in order to excel as a person and an athlete. Sometimes that may be an iron fist, and sometimes that may be a more sensitive approach.

Regardless of what your athlete needs to achieve new heights, they always need you to believe in them. Once your player feels that you have given up on them, most often they will lose confidence and perform worse. Even if you are in a sport with a militaristic culture, that does not mean that you cannot tell your players that you believe in them. A simple statement like "even though you're not playing a lot right now I believe in you" can go a very long way.

The goal is always to sustain or regain confidence. In a worst case scenario, when confidence is not attainable for a time, simplicity is key. Sports are simple. Hit the ball. Throw the ball. Catch the ball. Do not make things too complicated. Bring everything back to the basic elements. Stop overthinking and stop guessing what your opponent is or is not trying to do. Focus on just doing your job the best you can.

Narcissism

Some readers of this book may be familiar with the term narcissistic personality disorder (NPD). This is a psychological illness in which a person views themselves as being greater in some way than they actually are. Many of you, I'm sure, are now thinking of people in your life that this may describe. However, please note the definition provided. It is an individual who thinks they are better than they *actually are*. Because of this particular definition, it would be very hard for LeBron James or Michael Jordan to be diagnosed with NPD. This is because they actually are the best at what they do! Sure you might find them obnoxious, intolerable, or overly cocky at times, but that is not abnormal given this definition. Are they actually as good as they think they are? Yes! They pretty much are. If Michael Jordan convinced himself he was a great baseball player, then we might have an actual issue.

Narcissism is a very relevant issue in professional sports. You may be tired of seeing wide receivers or cornerbacks sing their own praises. For them, the question is: are they really as good as they think they are? Maybe the bravado is just a show and internally they are insecure about declining skill or increasing age. For them, the distinction between confidence and narcissism can be blurred.

What is extremely common among those that cross the line into narcissism is the tendency toward narcissistic injury. This happens when a person with NPD is faced with hard evidence that they are not as great as they think they are. At first, coping with narcissistic injury may be met with denial. The narcissist might say: well, I only got beat three times today because I didn't sleep well last night, or my speed is only tailing off because it's the end of the season and I'm tired. However, eventually most people with NPD are forced to

cope with narcissistic injury. The results are often very hard to watch and are marked by a wide range of reactions including depression, rage, and confusion.

Retirement is hard for most people that I see in my office, even if it is not related to sports and even if it comes after a long and successful career. We as human beings are meant to struggle, work, and overcome. When a person struggles and has ambitions over 40 years and then has them taken away all at once, it can be a traumatic experience that leads to frightening existential questions like: what is my value? What am I contributing to the world?

Relate this same issue to the professional athlete in retirement and the problem is only compounded. Pro athletes are people who have grown accustomed to having tens of thousands of people cheering for them. They have a constant flow of money coming in. They are the best of the best at what they do on the planet. They get the best medical and nutritional advice and attention. They are signing autographs for adoring fans. Then suddenly, it is all gone. They find that they are no longer the best of the best. The money dries up. Nobody is cheering for them. They often have no direction or plan. Further, their retirements often begin in their thirties rather than their sixties or seventies. Further complicating matters is the fact that many of them are living with chronic pain or cognitive problems resulting from their playing days.

Even for those professional athletes who do not fall victim to narcissistic thinking, the transition to life after sports can be brutal. This is an area where navigating the line between narcissism, cockiness, and confidence is of the utmost importance.

Cinderella Man James Braddock

Perhaps no athlete in history has experienced so much repeated failure followed by such extreme success as James Braddock. Painful losses and injuries can take a major toll on one's confidence. In fact, Braddock's performance became so poor that he was forced to leave boxing to work as a longshoreman. Braddock eventually got his chance at a comeback, winning the heavyweight championship in a stunning upset. He continued to believe in himself and his past successes despite what everyone around him was saying. This is the true definition of maintaining confidence and standing tall.

6   Go Beyond Mental Toughness
       (Mental Endurance)

The men's lacrosse team was stacked with talent. This was the team that would not only win conference, but also a national championship. Regardless of what NCAA division you are in, this is a tall task. However, this recruiting class had been the best in the program's history. The incoming group was packed with junior college and high school standouts. The juniors and seniors had already proven their effectiveness. They had come close in the past but had never reached the top of the mountain.

The team seemed to have the right attitude across the board. They genuinely liked each other and felt that they had the ability to beat anyone they faced. There were also players on the team that had a shot at playing professional lacrosse—particularly impressive considering this was not a Division 1 program. The potential future pros included two seniors: Steve, the team's starting goalkeeper; and Paul, one of the team's highly talented returning attackmen. They took very different routes to get where they were.

Steve grew up in a wealthy area as a major sports junkie. He attended private schools throughout his life. Once it became clear that he was highly talented in lacrosse, his parents sought out a school that would give him the chance to excel. While he played every position as needed, he settled on goaltender because his coach felt it allowed him to have the greatest impact on the overall game. Steve never struggled academically, socially, or athletically. He was charismatic and happy, always with a smile on his face. He dated the same girl for 3 years—almost an eternity by high school standards. He was the type of kid who would be voted most likely to succeed in the yearbook.

Paul's background and life experiences were quite different. While he also grew up in a fairly affluent area with loving parents, things did not come easily to him. He was diagnosed with attention deficit hyperactivity disorder at a young age and put on stimulant medication. He seemed to do well for periods of time before the medication stopped working for him and he needed to switch to a new one. Nobody ever doubted that Paul's heart was in the right place, but he couldn't keep up in class. When his medication was not working well for him, he also became somewhat of a class clown.

His parents eventually placed him in public school, where he received accommodations for his attention deficits. Paul sat at the front of the classroom, had extra time on tests, and seemed to finally fall into a groove. He took up lacrosse in 9th grade and he loved it. In addition to his newfound academic adequacy, Paul's success in lacrosse helped him further fit in. This was especially important because, despite his kind nature, he was not considered "cool" by the other kids. Nonetheless, he found his place in school and was generally content.

In contrast to Steve, Paul did not have the grades to go straight into a reputable 4-year college out of high school. He settled for junior college, as it allowed him play lacrosse without making him feel as overwhelmed academically. After 2 years of hard work, he was able to transfer and play alongside Steve.

The lacrosse regular season went as planned with the team winning the conference championship. Steve and Paul played well all year. However, during the NCAA tournament both Steve and Paul were ruled out of their second round game and the team subsequently lost. It was an extremely disappointing end to a highly anticipated season. Steve became ill with food poisoning shortly before the game was to be played, while Paul suffered tendinitis in both knees that he could not tolerate any longer.

Despite their efforts, neither Paul nor Steve had the opportunity to play professional lacrosse. Granted, this was not Division 1, which would have made the likelihood of professional play higher, but these are two young men who were at least on the edge of being given a chance at playing at the highest level. While there are likely many factors that led to them being left out, their inability to play in their team's final game was undoubtedly a major factor.

There are many ways in which sports are fair. In baseball, if a batter reaches on an error and goes on to score, it does not count against the pitcher's earned run average. This is fair, because had the fielder made the play that they should have made, then the runner would never have reached base. In fact, if anyone reaches on an error with two outs, all subsequent runs are unearned. Again, this is fair.

Unfortunately, there are also many ways in which sports are highly unfair. Only a tiny percentage of high school athletes are good enough to play in any division of college sports. From there, only a tiny percentage of those college athletes are good enough to play at the pro level. This varies widely by sport. Scouting staffs are tasked with the extremely difficult job of finding a needle in a haystack. The one athlete in a huge group that can contribute to their organization in a positive way. Sure, if you are Mike Trout, then sitting out a game because of tendinitis probably won't change the fact that you are destined to play pro ball. However, for everyone else, it can make all the difference in the world.

The question here is, how badly do you want it? Really, how badly do you want it? Are you willing to play with knee pain if your trainer tells you that you won't reinjure yourself by playing? Are you willing to drag yourself to the pharmacy to take nausea medication so that you can stop throwing up long enough to play? If your answer is "no," then you are a normal person. One of the overwhelming majority of members of the population who thinks rationally about life and sports.

If you want to be a part of the tiny percentage of the population that plays pro sports, you have to be willing to give everything you have regardless of pain, nausea, disliking teammates, disliking coaches, or any other obstacle. This is beyond mental toughness, it is a mindset that is etched into the mind of the potential professional athlete. Another question to ask yourself is: how much do I really like this sport? If you plan to go pro, you had better eat, sleep, dream, and breathe it. Doubleheader? No problem. Thirty-six holes today? Great. Two a days in the heat? Bring it on. Would it take an army to keep you off the field? If you hesitated even a little bit in answering this question, then you do not currently have the right makeup to play at the highest levels. Is it fair? Absolutely not.

In no other sport is this level of mandatory obsession more clear than in ice hockey. Every sport has a unique culture. A major component of the dynamic culture of ice hockey is playing through anything, especially in the playoffs. Patrice Bergeron of the Boston Bruins played Game 6 of the Stanley Cup finals with a punctured lung, broken rib, and separated shoulder. So the next time you think about not giving your best effort because you don't like who your coach paired you with for doubles, it may be time to look yourself in the mirror and reevaluate your priorities.

The Yips

While on the topic of mental toughness, it is important to include a discussion on the yips. The yips happen when an athlete is unable to do something fairly simple that they have always been able to do easily in the past. There are examples in almost all sports, but the issue is particularly prevalent in baseball.

One very memorable example comes from Chuck Knoblauch of the New York Yankees. He was an excellent defensive second baseman, even having won a Gold Glove as the best defensive second baseman in the American League. He also was an All Star and won multiple world championships with the Yankees. One day, seemingly out of nowhere, he was no longer able to make the throw from his position at second base to first base. This is the shortest throw from any position to first base on the baseball field. He worked with professionals with no success. He was eventually forced to move to other positions on the field.

Possibly the most famous case of the yips in recent baseball history is that of Rick Ankiel. He pitched well in his first season with the St. Louis Cardinals before falling apart seemingly out of nowhere during a playoff game. He gave up several runs and threw multiple wild pitches before being removed from the game. Ankiel was never the same and was no longer able to make it as a Major League pitcher. However, his story has a happy ending. Luckily, he was also an adequate hitter. He eventually finished out his career as an outfielder at the big league level.

As previously mentioned, the yips are not just isolated to baseball. Over the years, there have been countless athletes who could no longer make a tap-in putt, kick a short field goal, or make a free throw. Why does this happen? Is it a "mental" issue? Of course it is! Everything is a mental issue. People seem to forget that the brain is the origin of all actions other than reflexes. Even the most mundane sport-related activity requires the brain/mind to kick it into gear. The brain/mind controls everything the body does.

So then, the question arises: how do you fix the yips? In my work I have had the good fortune to spend time with a particular former professional golfer who could no longer make a putt from 2 feet. Sometimes the ball would go 10 feet past the pin, and sometimes it would go sideways. The one thing that was certain was that it would almost never make its way into the bottom of the cup. With this particular golfer, he had no history of psychological problems, no family history of psychological problems, no history of drug use, no medical problems, and an overall pretty normal life. After spending some time with him, it became clear to me that there was no underlying, deeply rooted psychological problem responsible for his issue. In his particular case, he was experiencing muscle memory gone haywire.

In our work, we restricted what his body could do so that it would be impossible for him to miss the putt. He was put into a jacket that made it impossible for him to move his arms and body in any way other than the exact line necessary to line up with the pin. This left only the force of his swing as a variable. Through hundreds of repeated putts, he eventually regained the appropriate muscle memory to sink his short putts. This is the one example of a success story of a person with the yips.

I have also had the good fortune to work with countless athletes who have had the yips. Each one has had a solution that was at least slightly different from the others. A baseball catcher, Manny, came to me with an inability to throw back to the pitcher. Throwing down to second base was no problem. However, when he tried to go to the pitcher, the ball would end up in the dirt, in the outfield, or even in the stands. This situation had a much different solution from the aforementioned golfer.

After spending a little bit of time with Manny, it became clear to me that he was suffering from frequent panic attacks. He complained that his heart would beat too quickly, he couldn't catch his breath, he felt nauseated, and he felt like he was going to faint. This problem was present across a range of areas in his life. They occurred when he was getting ready to take a test, when he was going to talk to a girl he was interested in, and most dramatically when he was stepping on to the baseball diamond.

Manny recalled that the problem began when he first left his home to go to college. These were the first games he had ever played in his life that his father was not present. It seems that he did not realize it, but his father had become a security blanket for him. He was never really able to understand the full positive effect that his father's presence had because he never had to play without him. Now, without his father, Manny's body felt so uncomfortable to him on the baseball diamond that he could not make a simple 60'6" inch throw.

Before the season, Manny had been cleared medically to play, and we had medical documentation to show that his heart was completely healthy. This gave us the opportunity to work together on his panic attacks. Unfortunately, trying to prevent panic attacks from happening is extremely difficult, if not impossible. In fact, one common feature of panic attacks is that the fear of future panic attacks causes new ones to come. It's a situation a little bit like being stuck in a finger trap. The more you struggle, the worse it gets. With panic, the path of least resistance is generally best. Because it can be nearly impossible to prevent a panic attack, the safest way to get past them is to embrace them. How do we embrace panic? By forcing the sufferer to have them more frequently. This in turn makes them feel normal in time.

Communicating this course of action did not make Manny enthusiastic about treatment. In fact, he asked if there was any other way to work on the issue. However, from a behavioral standpoint, this type of exposure is the gold standard for treatment of panic attacks. First, we began by having Manny breathe through a straw. After only 10 seconds or so, his heart rate increased. I then had him jump up and down until he was in full panic mode. We then spent time talking through what he was experiencing. Over time, he became accustomed to the feeling of panic to the point where he almost didn't care whether he was panicking or not.

Next, we transferred this same practice onto the baseball diamond so that he could get used to carrying out all of his normal baseball activities while experiencing this heightened level of anxiety. While it was difficult at first, he quickly found a way to play catch with me while experiencing panic. Over the course of a few days, his throws became more accurate. This then led to him practicing with his teammates and making accurate throws once again. This is not to say that he did not experience anxiety on the field anymore. Rather, if he did, he just didn't care much.

The case of our previously mentioned golfer and Manny represent two opposite ends of the yips spectrum. The golfer's issue was simply related to muscle memory. It required us to rewire his brain, in a sense, so that it sent previously learned messages to his body once again. Manny's issue, on the other hand, was more psychological, involving problematic anxiety. In either case, as is always true, the mind controls the body. As such, unless it is a matter of sheer strength, almost all athletic problems have a mental component.

Mental Toughness Through Tranquility

When we think of mental toughness, we often think about grit, strength, and endurance. However, mental toughness often involves putting one's mind in a calm, tranquil state. This is especially true in the clutch. Imagine a basketball player shooting two free throws at the end of a game. Hit one and you tie; hit two and you win. Is this a time for the shooter to grit his teeth and get intense? For the overwhelming majority of basketball players, this is not the best approach. The idea of hitting the game winning free throws can get you charged up. However, in this circumstance, getting riled up is likely not the best choice.

In this sort of situation, serenity equals toughness. Simply fighting the urge to excitedly celebrate the opportunity to win the game is a part of the challenge. On the road in the National Basketball Association (NBA), in this sort of situation there would be thousands of fans screaming directly in front of you as you attempt the shots. In addition to this craziness, you are faced with the harsh reality that these shots may cause people to see you as a "choke artist" or as clutch.

Part of the beauty of this situation in a sport like basketball is that you can step away from the free throw line and collect yourself. There is absolutely no reason to approach these free throws any differently from ones you took in the first quarter. Ultimately, our goal is to believe that we are not trying to be clutch. It's just another opportunity to hit free throws just like any other.

Take a look at the expressions on the faces of some of the greatest clutch athletes of all time: Michael Jordan, Joe Montana, and Jack Nicklaus. In those clutch moments, they almost look like they're dead inside. They are emotionless. It's as if they are the only ones in the stadium or at the course who cannot appreciate the gravity of the situation they are facing. You will not see any panic or fear. Interestingly, psychopaths generally do not feel emotions such as empathy. When they commit crimes, they do so in a matter-of-fact way, often without any remorse. This is how the clutch athlete works (obviously, I am not saying that clutch athletes are psychopaths). They are emotionless and enjoy

the process of putting their competition out of their misery. To put it in a cruel way, it seems like they almost enjoy crushing the dreams of the players on the other team.

This aspect of mental toughness only further underlines the importance of pregame routines, as we have already discussed. Here, the benefits are clear when it comes to using imagery to see the game play out in your mind before it happens. Think about watching a horror movie. One of the many tactics that filmmakers use to keep you frightened is the element of surprise. Everything outside of a person's home is quiet, and suddenly a zombie pops us screaming in the direction of the camera. This leaves the audience terrified and hiding under their blankets. However, the next time you watch the movie, it's much less scary and intimidating because you know what's coming. Obviously, before a game we cannot know exactly what situations we will be put into. Nonetheless, there is a tremendous benefit to using imagery, as it makes the clutch situation less intimidating because we have already had the benefit of seeing it in our minds.

Mario Lemieux

One of the all-time greats, Mario Lemieux led the Pittsburgh Penguins to two Stanley Cup championships as a player. When talking about mental toughness, it would be negligent not to bring him up as a player to look to. Lemieux was considered one of the best players in the league when he was diagnosed with Hodgkin's lymphoma. Having already accomplished so much in his career, he had every reason to hang up the skates when he was diagnosed. However, at the conclusion of his treatment, he returned to the ice and led an extremely dominant Pittsburgh team once again.

Lemieux also endured chronic back pain, something that is exceedingly challenging in a sport where one is most often hunched over a hockey puck. In addition to his aforementioned cancer treatments, he underwent multiple back surgeries and still returned. He embodies the type of player who is not just mentally tough, but is something more. I imagine that if he broke a leg during a playoff game, he would try to put his skates on his hands so that he could get on the ice. When you think about your own level of grit, look at Lemieux and ask yourself: is that me?

7 Be Flexible (Openness to Change)

From a very young age, Eva was always confident and stubborn. Her mother and father found her to be much more challenging than her older sister for this reason. Eva wanted things her way. This tendency caused her to have problems making friends in school, as none of the other children wanted to play with someone so focused on themselves. When her sister went on play dates, Eva remembers staying at home and playing alone.

Growing up in France, Eva came from a family that had no athletic pedigree whatsoever. She herself, however, became interested in swimming and diving at a very young age after watching the Olympics on TV. Despite their limited experience in the sports world, Eva's parents were happy to support her enthusiasm and began swimming lessons. Eva knew how to swim from a very young age, but she felt that doing so competitively was a completely different level of fun.

In school when Eva refused to lose, it cost her friends. However, swimming provided the outlet that Eva needed. It was a place where she could be bullheaded, refusing to lose, and be rewarded for it. People around her in the swimming world did not mind her stubbornness as much because she seemed to win so frequently. She was a natural, and her coaches never felt a need to drastically alter much of what she was doing. The more and more she succeeded, the more flexible she became in other areas of her life. It seemed that this change in other areas was because she was satisfying her need to win in the pool. Eva became a great example of a troubled child who benefited from sports.

Much of Eva's early success in swimming was because she grew at a younger age, and had more size and muscle mass than most peers. Around the age of 16, her growth slowed and other competitive swimmers her age grew faster and stronger. This led to poor finishes that seemed to get worse with time. Her futility in swimming then began affecting her life out of the pool, and her parents saw a side of her that they had not seen in years. Eva would tantrum and refuse requests from her parents. These problems were surprising as her parents felt that they had been resolved years ago.

Eva is a great example of how strong character is of the utmost importance. Sure, if you are naturally an elite talent, one in a million, people might put up with your rigidity and poor character for a time. However, if you follow the so-called divas in pro sports, you know that the willingness to put up with poor character, high-end talent has its limitations. Attitude problems cost stars large amounts of money because teams feel that their makeup would interfere with positive team culture. Selfish attitudes can even cost athletes years of their career.

There are many character traits that are important in athletics. Humility, confidence, ability to focus, grit, and loyalty are just a few. However, among the most important are flexibility and conscientiousness.

Flexibility is the willingness to be open to new ideas. No matter how great you are or how long you've been playing the game, there are many people that know more. Sometimes, great concepts and methods for improvement come from the least likely sources such as younger teammates or inferior players. Why? Because that inferior player may have had to work harder than most to get to where he is. When athletes are unwilling to change their growth becomes stunted. Take advice from anyone you can get your hands on. Don't write anyone off. This advice refers to both mental and technical aspects of your sport. Nobody has reached a point in their athletic career where the right advice would not benefit them. This includes the best of the best. With competitive sports, everyone is constantly pushing to get better. You are either going forward or you are going backward. Nobody stands still. If you do not seek counsel from those around you then someone else will and will eventually take your spot. If you have doubts about the advice you receive ask a trusted source. Get as many opinions as you can. This is crucial because ingraining bad technique into muscle memory can set an athlete back a long way.

However, the question remains, how do I balance flexibility with confidence? If I am constantly changing the way I approach things then how can I be confident in what I'm doing? The simple answer lies in whether or not you are willing to accept that you may be doing things the wrong way. You may need help. If you consider change and help from others as a necessary part of the equation in improvement, then you are thinking the right way. If you believe that sometimes it's best to close your mouth and open your ears, then you are on the right side of that line as well.

Savvy sports teams are always looking for conscientious players. Sometimes, these are called "glue" guys or girls. Conscientiousness at its core is a tendency to do the right thing. One important aspect of conscientiousness is how you relate to your teammates. As an athlete you have to be personally ambitious, but are you ambitious at the cost of your teammates? Would you rather play than sit on the bench if you know it gives your team the best chance to win?

In general, when you think about conscientiousness you should think about others. Are you taking the needs of others into account? If a younger teammate comes to you with a question are you going to take the time to answer it? Will it be a quick answer just to get them to leave you alone or will it be something that really helps them as a competitor? Believe it or not, helping others makes you better in a number of ways. First, it builds confidence knowing that you are a person that teammates turn to when they need help. The less help you give, the less likely they will be to come back. Second, it reinforces the things that you already know. As you advance as an athlete it becomes very easy to forget the simple parts of the game that got you to where you are.

Conscientiousness also comes in other forms. Are you organized? Do you show up to team activities on time? If your coach cannot count on you off the field it will eventually bleed into his or her feelings about you on the field. In order to be at your best, you have to have your act together in all areas of your life. Have there been great athletes who show up late and are inconsiderate? Sure! But no matter how great they are their careers would have gone even further with some thought and respect for the time of others. Being late should be completely unacceptable to you personally. Too many careers have been wasted because an athlete simply could not hold their lives together off the field.

If you travel for competition, conscientiousness also extends to sloppiness. Do you take care of your belongings so that they don't interfere with your roommate's ability to manage their belongings? Are you the person on the team that nobody wants to room with because you are not liked? Trust me. Even the seemingly unimportant things matter. When you want to be a part of an elite group that only a fraction of a percentage of the population belongs to everything matters.

Ego

Ultimately, much of what this chapter comes down to is your ego. Egos are our enemies in sports. Ego is that fine line that you cross when you take confidence too far. It hurts us in a number of ways. First and foremost, it makes us complacent. In hockey, the old saying is that a two-goal lead is the most dangerous lead in hockey. Why? Because it's just enough to make you comfortable with where you are. It's a place where you are proud of yourself and are more than happy to coast through the rest of the game. It's not as though people that are up by two goals actively choose to be less diligent. It's human nature. Having a lead subconsciously creates a level of comfort. It takes character to hold a lead.

To that end I would argue that most leads, not just the two-goal lead, are dangerous. Being up seven games in July is often not a good situation for a baseball team. You look down at your opponents. You take your foot off the gas and by the time you remember how to put it back on, it's too late. Your ego has gotten the best of you. You've become fat, dumb, and happy. This fat, dumb, and happy trend happens both on a team and a personal level.

Another way that ego hurts us is that it makes us unlikeable. No matter how good you are nobody wants to hear you boast. Teams often weigh a player's skill against how much of a headache they are because of their ego and the fact that they think they are invincible. Keep in mind that once you get to the highest levels, everyone is watching and judging you. Not just your game but your "makeup." If you treat your athletic trainer poorly it absolutely will come back to bite you. Both pro and amateur scouts frequently talk to anyone they can get their hands on. Everyone wants to be as sure as possible about their investment. It doesn't matter if that investment is a $20,000 scholarship or a multimillion-dollar contract. Treat everyone kindly. If you need it relayed in terms of dollars and cents then think of yourself as a stock. If you have a negative interaction with an equipment manager or assistant coach then your value drops.

In golf in particular, one would think that character doesn't matter. If you have the best score in Q-school, then you get your tour card. If you have a strong enough round, then you qualify for the final rounds of the tournament. Unfortunately, even in golf this is not always the case.

I have had the benefit of working with many great golfers in my career. There is one in particular that sticks in my mind and I see as a tremendous waste of talent. Meet Cara. Cara was born into poverty in Arizona and early on never had any aspirations of being a great athlete. Even at a young age she felt like she was just trying to survive. Her mother was addicted to drugs and her father was in prison for as long as she could remember.

She bounced around in foster homes and never really felt that she was a part of a family. She was even abused at one of her foster homes. By the time she reached the age of 12, she was finally placed with what seemed to be a caring family. They were a working-class family that seemed to have everything she could have needed. They were certainly not rich, but she had a bed, food, and consistency for the first time. Her foster father loved golf. They would take his 30-year-old clubs to the driving range when they wanted to spend time together. It was a great way for them to bond.

In time, maybe because of her positive associations with the sport, Cara decided to get a job at the driving range so she could be around the game more. She got better over time until eventually her father decided to buy her the best set of clubs he could afford. For the first time in her life, she found something she loved. She struggled academically and golf provided her with confidence for the first time. She played for her high school team. This gave her a huge sense of pride because she finally found something that she was better than the other kids at.

Cara got so good that she started getting offers from major colleges. When she finally decided on one, she was the best at her school immediately. Throughout her time she was consistently the one seed at tournaments. Every club in her bag was better than the next best golfer on the team. On paper, she would seem to be a lock to play at the next level.

One thing stood in Cara's way, however, and that was her attitude. Cara had a big heart off the course. She was a good person, but was never a team player. She felt that golf was an individual sport and she didn't owe anything to her teammates or coaches. In her mind, just the fact that she was improving the team's scores should have been enough for them. During practices, Cara always did her own thing. Her coaches felt helpless to change the situation. They wanted to keep her happy so that she didn't transfer, which is something she threatened repeatedly. During practices she separated herself from the team. If they were at the driving range, then she would go to the putting green. She did whatever she wanted to because she was the best.

Cara also had no interest in helping other players on the team when they were struggling. Other players never dared going to her for assistance, although she probably could have elevated their games if she cared to. This pattern of selfish behavior in golf continued despite the best efforts of coaches, friends, and mental health professionals. Cara's early life experiences seemed to have really shaped her attitudes later in life. Early on, all she wanted to do was survive and care for herself. She didn't have the ability as a child to think about anyone else's needs because she was so busy tending to her own. Nobody was there to take care of her, so she focused on herself.

Unfortunately, this attitude stuck with Cara. She viewed the world as a dangerous place, one in which she always had to put herself first. If she didn't this could make her vulnerable, something she would never allow. She saw golf as her path to survival and she was determined to make sure that nobody took it from her.

When she graduated, Cara began setting herself up for her professional career. Unfortunately, the Ladies Professional Golf Association (LPGA) does not pay anywhere near what the PGA does. She knew that this left her with little margin for error. When she tried to find a sponsor she repeatedly came up empty. Her game on its own merits likely would have warranted a sponsor. However, her attitude preceded her wherever she went. Companies did not want to be associated with an athlete that they felt would have a bad reputation. Without a sponsor she was unable to afford to travel to many tournaments. Ultimately, this forced her to leave professional golf for good. Please see this as a cautionary tale of how not to behave. People at the next level are probably not going to be interested in working with someone with a terrible attitude.

Curt Schilling

Whether you love Curt Schilling or you hate him, there is a lot to be learned from his career. If you have ever heard him talk about his early career, he will be the first to tell you that he did not manage himself well. He was the sort of

player who thought that he was good enough to get by with minimal preparation. He was the type of guy who thought he had all the answers and did not need any help.

This comes as a major surprise for some given what his attitude became later on in his career. He ultimately won multiple World Series titles and dominated on the mound. Curt will also tell you how a conversation with another, more respected pitcher showed him what it really takes to make it as a big leaguer. In the end, what benefited him more than anything else was the willingness to listen to people that had something to valuable to offer.

In the beginning of his career, Curt had all the talent in the world. The problem is that talent does not take you far enough. Even the best of the best need help. If Schilling had never sought help from others, it is extremely unlikely that he would have accomplished anywhere near what he did. There are so many ways that cockiness can stop you, but the inability to learn from those that have already been there is likely chief among them.

Conclusion

Elite athletics move quickly. As such, the seven habits must become second nature. It is important to constantly work to improve oneself mentally.

The most important mental skills in sports can be boiled down to seven concepts. While each concept contains within it a seemingly endless amount of information, the goal is to keep things as simple as possible. Elite athletics move fast. In order to keep up with this speed one must fight the temptation to overthink their approach. Everything has to be done at lightning speed. Understanding the seven habits is the easy part of being effective mentally. The hard part is going through them over and over again until you can use them with more ease. An athlete does not have time to think about mental skills during a play. To take it a step further, there is often not enough time to think about mental skills during a busy season. Therefore, the goal is to make them become second nature. These seven habits should be viewed as a journey with no destination. The more you practice them the further you will get. If you ever feel that you have completely mastered these skills, then it's time to start over.

Index

For Product Safety Concerns and Information please contact our EU
representative GPSR@taylorandfrancis.com
Taylor & Francis Verlag GmbH, Kaufingerstraße 24, 80331 München, Germany

* 9 7 8 1 0 3 2 4 7 5 8 3 7 *